The Process Mechanic™

A Self-improving Team Story
Robert Woodcock

IngramSpark

The Process Mechanic™, A Self-improving Team Story.

The story, all names, characters, and incidents portrayed in this production are fictitious. No identification with actual persons (living or deceased), places, buildings, and products is intended or should be inferred.

1st edition 2025

Library of Congress Cataloging-in-Publication Data

Woodcock, Robert W

The Process Mechanic™ - A Self-improving Team Story.

Library of Congress Control Number: 2025908014

ISBN: 979-8-9986828-4-1 (Hardback)

ISBN: 979-8-9986828-0-3 (Paperback)

ISBN: 979-8-9986828-2-7 (eBook)

ISBN: 979-8-9986828-3-4 (Audio file)

The Process Mechanic™, A Self-improving Team Story is a work of fiction.

Printed in the United States of America

For Maryjane, Bill, Laney, and Spencer

Contents

Introduction

"No Man ever steps in the same river twice, for it's not the same river and he's not the same man."

- Heraclitus

Executives and leaders, you find there's always something getting in the way. Your people and their teams have untapped potential. Your improvements do not take hold. Instead, people revert to old ways of doing things over time. You want them to adapt to new strategies, new goals, and a change in direction. Turn on a dime. See your strategies come to life!

You want them to create a predictable, steady flow of product value that your customers want to pay for and that contributes to the organization's bottom line.

Surprisingly, your Project Managers and Agile practitioners may be more like you than you know.

Agile, Change, and Project Managers, you lead from behind, working in the shadows, trying to be the CEOs of your teams. You do your best to remove roadblocks that get in the way of progress which are often the result of broken systems.

You toil in silence, serving two masters. You try to satisfy your leadership and inspire the people on your teams. You influence in secret, assessing the circumstances you find yourself in, adjusting to the situation. You try to make the best of your world and effect change. You dream about making an impact on the people and the company you serve. It is not easy. It can be a struggle. You wonder if it is even possible.

Developers, you want to come to a healthy environment every day where you can resolve problems, without the burdens of impediments or excessive meetings that have little value. You want to apply your engineering skills to create product solutions that address issues and make customers happy. Doing this is what makes you happy.

Simon Sinek once said, "Happy employees ensure happy customers,"

True agility is about being able to change direction quickly and create better outcomes. Achieving this requires interactions among individual leaders, engineers, and customers.

What you may not know is that happy engineers and teams need adaptability and flow to be predictable. Flow enables sustainable development. Roadblocks in the system interrupt the flow of valuable working code and frustrate developers worldwide.

You have seen these kinds of problems before. They are often problems you may not understand and cannot solve alone. The improvements seem barely out of reach. The question is, how did you react?

People, processes, and tools. Only one can solve problems without the others: people. Processes and tools only help them solve problems faster. It is important to be cautious not to overemphasize them. Not every framework, methodology, or tool is a wholesale fit for your company's situation and culture. Even Spotify, in its transformation use case, said not to take their Agile model and apply it directly to your organization.

So, what are we to do? Adapt! Figure out which process or tool is best to help your people solve problems in your context. It does not matter what you call it: Project Management, Agile, or Change Management, you can drive productivity *and* predictability to create high performing teams who make products we all dream of, that satisfy customers and contribute profits to your bottom line. It is possible!

This story is about a team that was not predictable or productive. Yet they wanted to create invaluable products and features and do good work.

How did they turn it around? The team developed an understanding of their circumstances to eliminate confusion and overcome multiple systemic problems.

They also used five key metrics in an Adaptability Scorecard to create a steady flow of value. It is a chart for everybody: executives, leaders, and teams.

They are now more predictable and effective, and have evolved into a self-improving team by adapting, while product quality and team health both improved dramatically. As a product development leader or developer, this is what you want.

Our saga begins with an overview of the problems Sully faces as he joins a team at Dominion.net, a huge telecommunications company in Austin, Texas where he finds obstacles at every turn, political pressure, and process challenges that are preventing his team's success. With a diverse cast of characters, will he be able to apply the right tool for the job at the right time?

You are about to find out.

This story is a fictitious account of how a team, using Agile principles, achieved unencumbered flow to become predictable and self-improving.

It would be impossible to believe if I had not lived it myself. The characters are fictional; the events are not. So, sit down, strap in, and buckle up. You are in for an incredible road trip!

May this story inspire you to view your situation and context objectively and self-improve. Enjoy!

Chapter One

THE RIGHT TOOL

Part One

"**I**f all you have is a hammer, everything looks like a nail."

– Abraham Kaplan

"Damn it! I busted my knuckles again!" It hurt like hell, and it was the third time he had hit the same spot, in the same way, today. His hands were black with dirt and grease, and he was on his back, doing everything he could to keep dirt and sweat out of his eyes.

He was precariously positioned in the gutter underneath the family's car, which had been parked with the passenger side wheels up on the street's curb. It was barely enough room to allow someone with a small frame to crawl underneath where he could access the part.

He was only 15 years old, and it was the first time Pops had let him do a repair on the family's '80's Chevy Malibu by himself. He was replacing the 305 cubic inch V8's starter on a Sunday morning. Pops was there to advise.

"Junior, you need to use the right tool for the right job. It requires patience. Those bolts require torque, and you've got to use the correct size 5/8" standard sized socket, not metric." "Also, it's a good thing your mom and sister went to Mass this morning, otherwise I'd have to chew your ass for swearing."

Pops had a clever, subtle sense of humor.

James Sullivan and his father were out front of the family's home on the second floor of a triple-decker (*tripl-deCAH*) off Fellsway, a working-class neighborhood outside of Boston, Massachusetts in the suburb of Medford (*med-PHah*). It is where Sully lived with his sister, mom, and pop.

Pops continued, "You found out that the adjustable crescent wrench wasn't the right tool when the wrench slipped and you smashed your knuckles the first time taking the old starter out."

Like most teenage boys, he was impatient and liked to learn the hard way. He would carry many of Pop's lessons with him throughout life.

"Okay, okay," Sully exclaimed as he crawled out from under the car, "I'll get the 5/8" socket and wrench."

He was determined to do the whole job himself.

His friends all called him Sully. It was a common nickname for someone from the Boston area whose last name was Sullivan. Sully was team-oriented and exceptionally disciplined from an early age, playing sports and joining his high school's Navy Jr.

ROTC program. It was here that he learned, if you are not 'five minutes early, you are late.'

The girls he met in school after moving to California for college had made fun of his thick Boston accent, so Sully worked at losing it. By his junior year it had practically disappeared.

One of them said, "Hey Sully, what happened to your accent? We thought it was cute!"

Sully was unsure and a bit confused by members of the fairer sex and still trying to get a grip on what they were all about. He could conjure his accent up at any moment, especially when he was kidding around with his buddies.

Back in his dorm room reflecting on what she had said, he smacked his forehead with his palm and said out loud, "You only need to be yourself,"

Another hard lesson.

Sully put himself through school, working in restaurants in San Francisco, where the pay was much better than at the part-time job he had had in high school. He graduated with a degree in Computer Science but would change his role shortly after graduating.

After more than 20 years working in California managing technical projects, Sully moved to Austin, Texas. He hoped to escape California's high cost of living and skyrocketing real estate prices. Now, he had found a place to live in Austin and landed a job during the middle of the COVID crisis.

He woke up and swung his legs off the side of the bed. He was confused about where he was; rubbing his eyes to clear the fog was useless. He glanced at his wristwatch, realized he could not see what time it was. The bedside lamp pierced the pitch-black night after he switched it on. He needed his glasses. Better, only his brain was still in a fog.

"Crap, it's 2:40 in the morning."

The fog started to lift.

"Okay, I'm in Austin and I start my new gig today." He turned off the lamp, removed his glasses, and rolled over to attempt to get a few more hours of sleep.

Sully started his day. He picked out a green striped shirt with a collar and a pair of jeans for his first day on the job. Even working from home, he wanted to appear and feel professional. He glanced at his reflection in the mirror to see how he looked.

Staring back were his clear, intense green eyes, evidence of his intelligence and occasional quick wit. A scruffy beard adorned his face, framed with straight medium brown hair that was styled and looked acceptable for now. Sully knew if it was cut too short, it would stand up straight. Of average weight, he stood six feet tall, was slightly athletic, and in his upper 40's.

It was a hot, humid day in early May of 2021. The six weeks of spring were quickly disappearing. Since the start of the pandemic in March of 2020, people were still learning how to avoid the virus and were settling into working from home.

To Sully, it felt as though the world was inaccessible.

Sully had a commute that was common for remote workers at the time. He rolled out of bed, splashed some water on his face, got dressed, poured some coffee, and went upstairs to his home office.

Sully had heard COVID and its social restrictions would be temporary, so his 'desk' in his home office was comprised of two folding white molded plastic tables that had been pushed into a V shape. They were inexpensive and ordered from an online retailer. He had a couple of widescreen monitors to go with his new laptop.

He was ready.

In those days, fresh off the interviewing circuit, his Project Management, Lean, and Agile certification plaques still hung on the wall behind him. That way he could show them off to his webcam audience.

His setup in a bedroom on the second floor also allowed him to look out the window at the neighborhood and street traffic, which were usually quiet.

Sully pondered his new role. *It's a bit of a step back.*

Despite the fleeting thought, he was eager to start his new Senior Scrum Master job at Dominion.net. His modus operandi was to jump into any new role with both feet.

Dominion had purchased several small independent start-up firms in the late 2010s in the home security and IoT, or "Internet of Things," space. It is a huge company, with well over 150,000 employees worldwide. With it came legacy divisions that employed an old school, command-and-control management style.

Many of Dominion's old guard managers had built internal empires, or cabals. The original purpose was to protect the people on the team from big company politics so they could focus on their work.

Somehow over time, the intent got muddled, influenced by periodic layoffs. Leaders became weary of losing team members and good people because of budget cuts. The idea was to stay under the radar, keep work as simple as possible, not innovative, not controversial, resist change, and hold the course. If they were invisible, perhaps no one in the group would get laid off in the next round of the coming year. They let fear lead them.

The team he would be working with was in Austin at one of the IoT firms Dominion had purchased. They were responsible for building Cloud microservices to connect home IoT devices to the internet for home security.

They had adopted Agile and Scrum.

I don't know what to expect, or what techniques or processes are in place, he thought to himself, *Will I be successful here?*

He felt excited and a bit nervous at the same time.

Although Sully had met his new manager during his interviews, he did not feel they had connected in a meaningful way. It was vital that he create solid working relationships with his manager, his teammates, and others who would be critical to his team's success.

Back in California, after five years with a data and analytics company, Sully started a new role at a medical device company in San Diego as a Program Manager within R&D.

He worked in the headquarters office. The two buildings each had two floors and were separated by an outdoor bridge. The entrance in the center was surrounded by several palm trees and tropical foliage, with an impeccably dressed live receptionist sitting inside the doors in an atrium. She also answered the incoming calls and directed their traffic.

The massive buildings included office space for various departments, executive offices, a manufacturing floor, and even a cafeteria where people ate food prepared by chefs. The two buildings were so long, it took 15 minutes to walk from one end to the other at a steady, determined pace. That is, if you were not stopped for a brief conversation along the way.

Sully remembered something his new manager, Brandon, had him do right out of the gate.

"I want you to meet all the department heads in the next two-weeks. Product, Engineering, *and* Customer Support, Manufacturing, and all the others."

The outcome of one of the meetings was unexpected.

Sully met with Bruce, the VP of Customer Service. Bruce's office was decked out with a solid mahogany desk with a matching credenza and bookshelves, along with a few padded armchairs for visitors. There were several plants next to the window and a few pictures of family.

His group was not only responsible for remote support, but they also had responsibility for servicing and keeping the medication dispensing machines housed in 80% of US hospitals operational and up to date. Lives depended on it.

Bruce stood about five foot, eight inches tall, was dressed in a pressed, white dress shirt covered by a nice navy-blue sport coat, supported by a pleated set of khaki slacks and a pair of polished brown leather shoes. He looked every bit an executive of importance in 2009.

Bruce was a nice enough guy. He played golf occasionally and had a family. After only 20 minutes of getting to know you chit-chat, Bruce had to take a call. As Sully was walking out of Bruce's office, he felt that Bruce had only agreed to their time as a courtesy.

On the other hand, Bruce had set up a ride-along for Sully with a couple of service technicians who had the task of updating the software of a device in one of the nearby hospital's emergency rooms.

Sully was curious about what went on out in the field.

On a sunny Wednesday, Sully arrived at the hospital in La Jolla, CA mid-morning and parked his silver VW GTI VR6. Overhead, the sky was blue like the color of a typical California pool, with a few cumulous fluffy, white clouds wandering somewhat aimlessly. He quickly realized there was no way he would find who he was looking for in the huge, ten-story hospital. It overlooked an enormous white temple with two opulent white spires that reached up into the sky and looked like, if someone were to climb them, they could speak with the heavens.

As he approached the main registration desk, Sully addressed the person dressed in scrubs, "I'm meeting technicians that are updating a medication station for you. They are in ER-521." implying he needed directions.

"Take the elevator around the corner up to the fifth floor and turn right."

Knocking on the open steel safety door to the ER, Sully introduced himself and observed what his two coworkers were doing. Both were dressed in conservative khakis and company polo shirts. The ER smelled like antiseptic and had just been sterilized. Pat, one of the service technicians, had already started the update on the machine. While they were waiting for it to finish, Pat and a coworker were openly gossiping about bad experiences they had had at other hospitals last week.

"I hope this new version works. We couldn't get an update installed over at Sharps last week. You should have seen people scrambling around trying to figure out some new policy or procedure. It was like the nurses didn't even know what they were doing, unbelievable!"

"Well, while you were doing that, I had the same trouble over at Scripps off University. What a nightmare."

Sully could not believe his ears, especially because one of the hospital's med-techs, in essence the customer, was in the ER with them!

Murphy's law was alive and in force in the small ER. The update failed. The service techs did not know what to do or how to approach solving the problem.

After reading the upgrade instructions which Pat assured had been followed 'to-the-letter,' Sully pulled his company-issued Blackberry out of its holster. He dialed a software engineer he had just met a few days earlier to help get the issue fixed.

It was a configuration problem. Together, they got it resolved, and Sully returned to the office.

Two weeks later, Sully had a follow-up with Bruce. It was Bruce's first opening.

"How'd it go, Sully?"

"They got stuck, and I called Mark, one of the dev's. He helped us get past a config issue that was causing the update to fail."

"Nice!" Bruce continued, "What else did you learn?"

"Well...I'm not quite sure how to put this." *Long pause,*

"While I was there, the service techs were sharing dirty laundry about another couple of updates that went badly at other hospitals. And they were doing it with the customer *in the room.*"

It was plain wrong.

"Frankly I was shocked that they were throwing us and other hospitals under the bus."

Bruce thought about Sully's report and said, "I know exactly what to do. We have an all-hands conference in a few weeks. I'll bring it up."

Bruce did. Sully had heard it was a major topic of discussion at the conference, and that Bruce, being the class-act he was, did not specifically call out who was guilty. Pat knew, regardless.

Wow, Sully thought, *I'm already having an impact!*

Sully quickly got a reputation as a problem solver and for speaking his mind.

Brandon's advice to get to know the people he would be working with early on proved to be an incredibly smart thing for Sully to do. In the long run, it paid off in a big way.

It would pay off at Dominion, too.

First things first, Sully thought.

He wanted to better understand the problems his new team were facing.

After a couple of weeks, Sully started to get his feet under him. He was getting to know his teammates and had built relationships with others he would work with indirectly at Dominion.

One of his new colleagues, George, a Distinguished Engineer and Architect with Dominion, explained Dominion's strategy to Sully, to make home security available to broadband customers.

George had short gray curly hair and was in his sixties. His sky-blue eyes bulged as though they wanted to jump out of his head. He typically wore an untucked polo shirt over cargo shorts that were comfortable and loose fitting. He is extremely intelligent, and an adept problem solver.

Dominion, one of the top five telecoms in the world, wanted to develop a new market for cutting edge 'do-it-yourself' home security by offering devices and technology for a nominal monthly fee. The people working on developing the technology were only several hundred or less than one-tenth of one percent of the total company.

George explained the company's strategy, "Once they adopt a few devices and use them for home security, customers become sticky."

"Sticky?" Sully asked curiously, "What makes a customer 'sticky,' George?"

"The more connected devices customers have, the more difficult it is for them to switch to a different internet provider. So sticky customers help Dominion retain its customer base."

"Why?"

"Because switching providers means setting up each of your IoT devices all over again. It would be painful for the customer."

"Will we be able to pull it off?"

"That's why we're here," George replied.

Sully understood. It was a competitive market, and switching providers was commonplace. This was a way to incentivize customers to stay, even if it was a little blackmail-ish.

Could they pull it off? The strategy seemed sound. They ought to be able to, except...

Other large publicly traded companies Sully had worked for in the past had tried to develop new technical products. A couple succeeded, while most failed miserably.

The same medical device company Sully worked with in San Diego had tried to reinvent their flagship product. The legacy product was nearly impossible to maintain, having been written for a MS–DOS operating system, 25 years before. The developers referred to its code as 'spaghetti.'

Twelve attempts were made over as many years with no success. It was not for lack of motivation.

Big company politics made it nearly impossible to make decisions or any progress on the new version. Previous attempts were canned due to budget cuts or frequent changes in strategy and focus. They even tried isolating the v12.0 team in their own building off campus. To make matters worse, vice presidents, not designers, were arguing over the cabinet's exterior color and design!

Sully questioned, *Would Dominion be the same?* And wondered if they would eventually find success.

Was there a chance at Dominion? Perhaps there were factors at work he did not understand as the newbie.

As for the rest of the group at Dominion in Austin, Sully was surprised to discover that the leaders had an Agile mindset. It was quite unusual, since many of the meetups he had attended before joining had one consistent, nagging question: how to get leadership to adopt an Agile way of thinking. It was strange indeed.

After getting to know his new team members a bit, Sully gauged the team's morale was at an all-time low. They were rushed, confused, and ineffective. They did not know what to do, did not understand the work, and lacked focus. The only two developers who were able to stay on point got the work done consistently. The rest were clearly frustrated.

While things may have appeared bleak, the people on the team were skilled engineers and engaged in their work. That is, whenever they found work that could be completed. They all had good intent and *wanted* to be productive. They paid attention to the results of their work and were accountable and committed. The teammates also did not back down if they had an alternate or opposing viewpoint, when they discussed solutions as a group.

Sully thought, *It's evident they trust each other.*

It's something else. Maybe the problem is in the process, Sully concluded.

He certainly did not want to be responsible for one of 'those'

Agile transformations he had heard about that failed.

Once he had gotten into the groove of daily stand-ups and the rhythm of the Sprints with his new team, Sully quickly learned there were issues, some bigger than others, that he would need to deal with. Communication and collaboration amongst the team members was difficult and half the team was off-shore, roughly a 12-hour difference.

18

In turn, some team members did not understand the work to be done, and there were multiple dependencies on someone outside the team that caused progress to come to a complete standstill. Additionally, the way deployments were coordinated, occasionally the working code was flat out lost!

Sully wondered if he had what it would take to right the ship.

Chapter Two

PRY BAR

"H appy customers start with well-defined requirements."

– Anonymous

The software engineering manager was harried as
he emerged from behind a conference room door,
in a rush to get to his next meeting, the second of
many that day. It was 8:55am and he was already
overwhelmed and exhausted. As an engineer, he was
frustrated. Things had not gone as he would have
liked. As a newly minted manager, he was doing the
best he could.

He grappled with a delicate balance, doing things correctly in the best way possible, or compromising the
solution so they could make some arbitrary timeline.
It is a common yin-yang that most developers wres-
tle with.

In the end, the timeline usually won out. The higher
ups, once engineers in their distant, forgotten past,
usually made the call. This, even though the people
who best understood the problem at hand, had the

best information, and labored on the front lines were rarely consulted.

Sound familiar to you?

This was a few months after Sully had started at Dominion, and after people started to work from the office one or two days per week. They called this mix of working from home and the office a hybrid work model. If someone felt the slightest bit sick, they would sequester themselves at home. There were even occasional social events, COVID-free friends gathering for a meal and game nights. Progress.

Dominion's office occupied the fifth floor of a non-descript grey building near the Pennybacker bridge, a through-arch design spanning Lake Austin. Sully and his colleagues sat in a cube farm, each cubicle separated by four-foot-tall grey acoustic walls. It was kind of plain. At least the cafe had a few vending machines and a wall of windows to view the Colorado River during lunch breaks.

In an effort to liven things up, they had named the larger conference rooms after local festivals. The smaller rooms received the names of local food trucks that were popular in Austin.

Sully bumped into Ganesh, the software engineering manager and Sully's peer, in the hallway. They were surrounded by a cube farm, with a conservative, short blue carpet underfoot designed for high use and longevity. It was a cloudy day outside, and Ganesh was rushing to get to the team's requirements refinement meeting.

"Headed to the refinement meeting?" Sully asked.

"Yes, and I have another meeting right after."

On its own, Scrum added meetings to everyone's calendars. Sprint planning, daily stand-ups, requirements refinement sessions, Sprint review, and a Sprint retrospective were the typical Scrum ceremonies. It was important that they were all valuable time spent.

At least Dominion, whom he blamed for his current predicament, saw fit to provide Ganesh some help by hiring Sully, the new Scrum Master.

In his mid-40's, Ganesh had short dark hair slightly graying at the temples, a moustache, and glasses. Ganesh usually dressed in a smart, collared shirt, perhaps in a blue or gray tone, with well-fitting trousers. After he migrated to Silicon Valley from India, he secured a master's in computer science (CS) and machine learning (ML), and certifications in Cloud Architecture and IoT.

In addition to being the team's manager, Ganesh also played the role of the team's Product Owner, representing the team's customer, a completely different skillset. It was unusual and awkward at times.

The dual roles caused Ganesh inner conflict; they were often at odds with each other. Amid the confusion, he still somehow managed to maintain his composure.

On top of his emerging dual personality and back-to-back meetings, Ganesh also had the responsibility of managing the 15 engineers on the Cloud team. He rarely smiled and was constantly in a rush, as if he was consumed with twenty confusing things all at the same time.

It was all too much to bear. Like many engineers-turned-managers, he wondered if he would have been better off returning to developing only. He reflected on better days when he had the time to focus.

No wonder the team was disorganized. Worse, he doubted if his large Cloud team could perform.

Sully's role as Scrum Master was not an engineering one, it was more of an organizer and process improvement role. The team reported to Ganesh, who was Sully's peer, while Sully reported to another manager with a couple of other Agile practitioners.

Where do I start? Sully thought.

It looked as though he would get little to no help from Ganesh, who was battling his own demons. Sully decided to start with an assessment of the situation and its causes, a technique he learned in his Lean Six training.

Why was the team's collaboration strained?

Aside from the 12-hour time difference the two halves of the team had to contend with, work stalled in the middle of the Sprint.

Time. The team members would get together virtually or in a conference room in the Austin office to refine requirements for the work to be done in the next iteration.

The team's requirements refinement meeting occurred every Friday in one-hour sessions starting at 9:00 am Central. More than half the team was virtual, the ones who had ventured into the office including Ganesh and Sully took seats around the conference table in 'ACL.' The conference room was named after one of Austin Texas' famous festivals, Austin City Limits.

Sully fiddled with a few buttons on the controller to connect the virtual audience. ACL was one of the larger conference rooms, it had a long table and had two video monitors at one end, one for displaying people that were online, and one for displaying a shared screen. In the middle of the table sat a device that allowed the remote team members to hear and be heard, even though that was sometimes difficult. There was also a whiteboard that could be shared with the remote audience. It was a pretty slick setup.

The meeting's goal was for every team member to gain some understanding, maybe 70–80%, of what needed to be done and to put forth ideas as to how to accomplish it. This was accomplished by asking questions and discussing possible approaches. There was rarely enough time. More than half the team members' cameras were turned off in Microsoft Teams, their video conferencing software.

Ganesh said, "To start, let's review ticket 3728."

"We need to connect the adapter for the new doorbell into the system so it can be connected to the app for the mobile team to do their front-end work," he highlighted what was needed.

He suggested, "How about we create a new API?" referring to an Application Programming Interface.

Ganesh nobly wanted to discuss the approach, or how to, with the developers to get their ideas, however, if two or three people were debating a solution, no one else could get a word in edgewise, even Sully.

In the end, Ganesh usually dictated the solution and how to implement it to the team because they always ran out of time.

To make matters worse, there were people on the call who had unanswered questions. There was never adequate time to listen to all the questions and address them thoughtfully.

The meetings ran over, and people would drop off the call without so much as a word.

It was also Friday night at around 9:00pm for people attending remotely offshore. The late-night calls interrupted precious family time and rest.

Not nearly enough time for each person to understand and be ready to make progress in the next two weeks, Sully thought, *we need more time.*

They were lucky if they made it through more than two to three tickets in each session.

For the oversized team of 15 people, there was hardly enough fully refined work ready to start in the next Sprint. Tickets that had not been given time for Q&A and forethought, and were not well understood, were assigned to one of the team members in the next Sprint anyway. It was a careless thing to do and painful to watch.

He continued his observation, ...*and it causes work to come to an abrupt stop after work has started.*

Then, because they want to work, the dev's look for something else they can complete which leads to frequent task switching, risking more and more defects.

More defects to fix. More time wasted.

Sully considered a few options and after a day or two, decided to start with what he could influence or control. The low-hanging fruit.

The current process was excruciating and next to useless.

Sully's mind raced. So did his resolve. He felt that he had enough influence now to make an impact quickly.

He took a deep breath and concluded fixing the broken requirements process would be job one. It caused uncertainty, confusion, and a lack of alignment.

When Sully was first starting out as a Project Manager, his boss signed him up for Project Management training. The classes were held at an older two-story Best Western hotel on Shelter Island in San Diego, California. Even though it looked like it was in need of a few updates, the setting was unbeatable.

Tropical plantings were placed strategically around the property, and the front door faced the bay and the US Navy's North Island base. While sitting on a park bench one noon eating the ham sandwich he had brought from home, Sully watched the USS Nimitz, an aircraft carrier, meander by on its way to the dock. The warm breezes had a slight scent of the ocean and the beach, which left Sully completely relaxed. The restaurant out back had a view of multiple small, moored yachts. The setting was absolutely serene.

Sully liked the format of the Project Management prep course. It was set up for five sessions spread out over fifteen months. It was a great way to learn. He would attend a three-day or five-day class, learn a skill, go back to the office and apply the skill for two to three months, then return to class for the next round.

His instructor and new mentor was Scott. He was tall, with a short, military-style haircut and usually dressed in professional, office casual attire. He had years of experience and worked for Jet Propulsion Labs on a famous NASA project.

Scott introduced himself and the syllabus to the cohort.

"During the first week we'll focus on communication and requirements."

"Great communication is made possible by establishing good working relationships throughout the organization."

The class worked through the material and exercises on communication and collaboration, and the importance of it.

Halfway through day two, Scott introduced the topic of requirements.

"Everything starts here."

"Writing requirements is a way to document and communicate *what* is needed."

"Good requirements communicate 'what' the customer needs and 'why' it's needed," he said, *drawing air quotes.*

"Bad requirements violate the engineer's ability to solve problems creatively by telling engineers how to solve the problem using such and such methods or tools."

"That is the job of specs, or specifications! Specs are where engineers explain their design of *how* they plan to solve the users' problem."

A classmate raised their hand, "My company doesn't write requirements, we have 'user stories' that explain things in terms the customer would use."

Scott replied, "User stories are a newer form of requirements. It's a format used in Agile Methods. That's a whole different topic."

Having satisfied her question, he continued.

"Anyone ever danced with someone who is out of sync with the music or you?"

He asked half-joking while he pulled up a clip of Seinfeld's Elaine dancing onto the screen.

"It's like this," he exclaims, "Someone could get hurt!"

"I don't dance. This is why," he admits while chuckling.

"Requirements and Specs create kind of a dance between the what and the how. Each must communicate their intentions. The dance is not only communication, its intent is to also have an important collaboration between the people who own the what, and those who own the how." *Long waiting pause.*

Scott addressed the class, "Who can see this might create some conflict?"

A few people raised their hands.

"Why?" He picked Sully, who quickly sat upright.

"It seems like the Product Managers and Engineers, or what and how, would be at odds."

"Exactly," said Scott, "*the* goal is to have an exchange, to challenge each other's approach, and to come up with an even better solution together!"

"Here's the thing, you can't make it personal. Make it about the solution, otherwise, tempers will flare."

The class ran through some exercises the next day.

Scott summed up the class and closed them out with, "Remember, if your requirements process is broken, the solution the engineers develop will not solve the problem. The development process starts *here!*"

Scott was right, it was time to improve the Dominion team's broken requirements process.

If Sully could help improve the process, the dev's would have an opportunity to complete work and reduce the confusion associated with switching tasks. It could also have a positive effect on some of the impediments he had observed and the frustration the team exhibited.

Scott said something else that stuck with Sully, "In order to understand what the problem is, why it exists, and the approach to solve it, engineers need time to think about the best approach for solving the problem."

But how? The team reviewed work items for the first time, barely hours before starting a Sprint, and they do not have enough time.

Sully had an idea.

"What if we set up a couple of times for us to preview tickets and poke holes in them," he asked George and Ganesh.

Sully thought they understood the system the best.

"That way you would have more time to come up with an approach and anticipate the team's questions before the team does final refinement!"

They agreed to try it. George suggested, "Add Niko as optional, that way he can decide to attend if he has time."

Niko, short for Nikola, was a Senior SW Engineer. He was a master at keeping solutions as simple as possible. Niko earned a degree in Computer Science in 2006.

Niko usually wore slacks and a collared shirt, had short, thick black and gray hair, was clean shaven, and had smile lines when he grinned. Niko was in his middle 30's. He and his wife had two small children and lived in Austin. Niko had a slim build, and blue eyes. Originally from Bulgaria, he came with an understandable, yet strong accent.

While he had not been at Dominion for long, he had a thorough working knowledge of how all the Cloud components worked together across the complex technical system.

Sully had added two additional meetings for pre-refinement to their calendars for pre-refinement. Since it was only the four of them, things would be able to move quickly.

After a few weeks, things were humming along. The whole team was handling more tickets in final refinement and understanding of the work was increasing. The team was getting better about not pulling work in that had not been reviewed.

Better yet, more tickets were getting completed in each Sprint.

Once a few additional improvements were put in place and the team became more proficient, the four meetings would eventually be trimmed down to an average of fewer than two, an achievement which was huge in the meeting-heavy environment.

They needed to focus on doing a better job of defining requirements, then making the time to better understand them and what they needed to accomplish to meet their goals. The addition of the pre-refinements was worth every minute.

This was a big step that for now had a small impact. The team would have to wait, but it would pay off in a big way in the future.

A mechanic's pry bar is a versatile tool to gain mechanical advantage in tight spaces when dealing with stuck or difficult-to-access parts. It can also be used to align components, much like having good requirements.

Sully started to sense some animosity from Ganesh, as if he was losing his grip on some sort of control. It seemed he thought Sully was a competitor, rather than a collaborator.

We're not out of the woods yet.

Chapter Three

MITCHELL GUIDE

"Don't move information to authority, move authority to the information."

– L. David Marquet

Communicating across the globe was still an issue. Sully noticed that when a work item was ready for someone to test it at the end of the day in the US, someone on the offshore team tried to test it first thing their morning. Little progress was made until they could speak to the developer, usually more than eight hours later when the US started its day. If there was a defect in development, it took longer than two days to get it resolved.

Sully approached Aishwarya in her cubicle to help him understand what the situation was. Her cube was littered with a dozen different Wi-fi devices, from sensors to doorknobs to cameras, and all could be operated remotely using Dominion's phone app.

Aishwarya stood at five feet four inches, was petite, and in her early 30's. She had dark features, glasses, and longish, straight, dark brown hair. Her clothes were casual yet professional and loose fitting. Occasionally, she would wear a traditional Nepalese dress or skirt.

Originally from Kathmandu, Aishwarya migrated to the US in 2008 and earned a B.S. in Computer Information Systems from Texas A&M.

Now, Aishwarya was a Senior QA Engineer, having worked for Dominion for eight years. She was a mom of two energetic young children who, along with her husband, kept her extremely busy when she was not working.

Aishwarya was a master at writing test cases and test automation and had expertise in solving tricky technical challenges. Skilled at writing scripts in Python and Java to validate APIs, as well as Golang programming languages, she had even earned a Cloud Solutions Architect certification!

Sully asked Aishwarya, "What's your biggest headache?"

"At the beginning of their day, the two QA in India, are stuck. They cannot validate new work which was passed to them from the US the previous day. Unless they have something else to do, they are twiddling their thumbs," holding out her clasped hands to demonstrate.

"They have questions and must wait almost 12 hours until they speak to the developer in the US," she continued.

"Hmmm," Sully said, "that explains the delay."

Aishwarya then followed, "If there was a way we could get the dev's to document test steps, then it wouldn't matter who validated it."

Sully asked, "What do you mean by test steps?"

"We need information about how to set up for the validation and what to test, such as 'test the new code and other adjacent components the new code could affect.'

"Knowing that will help us get a start on resolving the time lag. We need to add that information to people who are running the test case."

Sully nodded, "I get it."

Sully flashed back to his two-day Scrum Master class which was held in a shared office space in Boston. It had been raining that day as Sully drove into the city from the burbs, and it was cold and damp outside on that September Saturday.

The conference room was set up with five folding tables with two chairs behind each facing the projection screen at the front of the room. There were several rolling white boards in the room; one had columns drawn on it to make it look like a Scrum board. The room had no windows and was on the dark side, illuminated only by about 12 low-watt can lamps in the ceiling.

Avram was the instructor and Sully's new guide.

Avram was a likeable character who had a medium build with a little extra weight on his frame, lively dark brown eyes, and thinning hair. Avram had years of experience in the development of technical products as a Project Manager, Scrum Master, and Agile Coach, and over 15 years as a Scrum Trainer.

Avram had said during one of the exercises, "Making information visible is a powerful way to communicate among the team and with stakeholders. It's why we visualize the flow of work items, or tickets using a Scrum board."

At Dominion, the team's user stories and tickets were represented in Jira, in the product backlog and on a Scrum board.

The people on the teams were constantly looking at tickets in Jira. Following Avram's teachings, Sully wanted to make the improvements visible on something they looked at multiple times a day. Adapt and overcome.

Sully translated Avram's advice into a possible solution, or way they could implement such a thing for Aishwarya.

"What if we could add a Test Steps field into each ticket, could that work?"

She agreed, "It's worth giving it a try."

Jira is a computerized system that reflects a more manual Agile and Scrum process. The name Jira came from the Japanese word, 'Gojira,' or Godzilla. The dev's at Jira's parent company, Atlassian, had nicknamed their defect tracking tool Bugzilla before developing Jira.

The Jira admins, or administrators at Dominion were an unusual, quirky bunch. Rarely did they ever have their camera turned on for video conference meetups.

Sully had even heard about one admin who had been traveling around the country in his car and crashing at his college friends' places when he was close by, working for Dominion out of local coffee shops and diners since the pandemic. Sully imagined them driving a beat-up car, perhaps an older, 1990's well-worn Toyota Camry with faded silver paint from years of accumulated road grime.

Dominion was such a large company, the admins performed certain duties because access had been restricted for one reason or another to the system's main users. Sully was one of those.

Sully submitted a request for help online in the admins' portal. After a few days, Sully started to reach out on Slack to the admin who was assigned to his ticket, to pester them into paying attention to his request. He was nice, and professional in his approach, knowing if he was not, he would certainly not get any help.

Finally on a call, Sully asked, "Could we add a text field for Test Steps? We need a place for the dev's to document test information on each ticket."

The Jira Admin said, "There's not a field for Test or Validation Steps. There is a custom text field for Test Data. We can't change the name."

"Great!" Sully continued, "Let's go with that. Please add it to all the tickets."

Sully heard the admin over the call as they typed on their keyboard, probably making a few commands and selecting a couple of buttons.

"Can we make this a mandatory step for any ticket moving from "In Review" to "In Test?""

"Whoa! One thing at a time," The admin responded, "Yes, we can make that happen."

Before the changes were made, Sully and Aishwarya discussed the proposed changes with the team, and how they would work. They all agreed to try it! Filling in the new Test Data field would be required when anyone moved a ticket to 'In Test.'

The solution promised that when the QA engineers offshore received a new work item, they could get started right away, and instead of waiting to speak to an engineer in the US, they would avoid any delays.

The next morning during their daily Scrum, Sully raised an after-topic to explain the new changes in their Jira tickets, why they were there, and how to use them.

Concluding the team discussion, Sully said, "These improvements are an experiment. That means we'll find out how they work for us and if you like them. They can be improved or could be removed altogether."

A week later, Sully asked Aishwarya, "Could you identify a great example of a write-up for test data?"

She did and reviewed it with the team, along with its finer points during the next stand-up.

Aishwarya said, "It explains the setup required for the test, gives some details regarding what to test, and includes other components that could be affected."

Sully chimed in, "This was written by Nitin."

Nitin was part of the offshore sub-team.

Sully continued, "What happened after you moved your ticket forward?"

Nitin said, "Aishwarya tested the ticket, and found an issue while I was asleep. I fixed it my next morning, and she validated it before I left the office."

"Wow!" Sully exclaimed, "that was quick!" emphasizing the experience for the team.

"Please share your ticket with everybody on the team, so they could use your write-up as an example."

Over the next few weeks, the team would get used to the new process. Some were more informative than others. Still, each developer did their best to communicate Test Steps. The improvement represented a twice-as-fast turnaround time in the validation step.

Sully rarely saw a user story or bug that had (null) or N/A written in the field.

We all know this situation: You need information and cannot find it anywhere or you must wait for someone else to provide it.

Now, they had the information they needed so they could proceed with validation, kind of like a mechanic that had to look up the procedure in the Mitchell manual on how to make a repair and ensure it was good.

It would have been easy for Sully to jump in and fix the test steps problem himself. In his experience, that only resulted in the return of the problem shortly thereafter. He believed it was important for the team to own the solution.

Now, the team was taking advantage of the time difference. It was an improvement, simply not enough.

Chapter Four

WAITING FOR PARTS

"There have been cases where I specifically decided to not work in an Agile way to achieve the best results. There isn't one size fits all, you need to pick the best approach given the context you're operating in. Agile is hot and popular, but that doesn't mean it is always the best solution."

– Maarten Dalmijn

The work to be done was still stalling in the middle of an iteration.

Sully stopped by Niko's cube, which looked like every other cubicle, except for a few pics of his kids and a couple of knick-knacks from home. He was busy writing code and stopped what he was doing when Sully approached with a quizzical look on his face.

"I noticed you pulled a new ticket into the Sprint," Sully asked,

"So what's the impact?"

Niko shook his head and said, "This other lower priority ticket will probably not get done. I'll try my best and we'll see what happens."

"Why?" Sully continued his inquiry.

"It's kind of a 'cart before the horse situation.' I had to stop working on the ticket in the Sprint because another one needed to be addressed first. The ticket in the Sprint had a dependency on a ticket in the backlog, we hadn't yet identified."

Sully replied, "I see. Any ideas why we missed it in the first place or how to fix the issue, so it doesn't happen again?"

"We need time to consider each ticket so we can identify dependencies ahead of time. Also, it may take a few days to track the dependency down."

"Most of the time, this happens because there's some unknown or dependency from a developer outside the team."

"It happened to me in the last Sprint."

Sully asked, "What teams?"

"It could be from firmware, mobile, even another platform team."

"If the other team has to complete something so we can start, and hasn't, then we are dead in the water."

Niko continued, "In addition, if what we need them to do isn't in their current Sprint, then we wait for them to hopefully complete it in the next Sprint,"

"We keep getting sidetracked. Dependencies make us stop what we are doing and try to resolve the issue.

More often than not, the work ticket sits idle while we wait for someone else."

Summing up, Sully said, "Yikes, that's frustrating. I've waited for somebody to complete their work in the past and almost missed my target. It was down to minutes and seconds. Sounds like we have a coordination problem."

Niko agreed.

More delays.

Niko had identified a big issue.

Avram was keen on making things visible. Sully knew that. He also remembered a conversation in class about dependencies.

Avram had taught, "A team and its scope of work *ought to* be self-contained. A self-organizing team is geographically located together and at least one of the team members has the skills required to complete the scope that is required. That stipulates there are different skillsets, user experience, mobile, software, firmware, and hardware engineers, that are all on the same team."

"How do we make dependencies visible," Judy, a student asked.

"If the team is self-organizing, then dependencies primarily exist within the team, and all tickets are actionable."

Judy fired back, "Yes, except my company has teams organized by skillset. There are separate teams for

UX/Design, Mobile, Cloud, and other development types."

Avram dropped his chin to his chest and let out a long *sigh*.

"Depends upon your situation. Large enterprises can still operate with the old-world ways of structuring...by expertise. These companies will struggle with adopting Agile."

"So how do I work with it? I'm not going to change a large company?" Judy looked bewildered.

"You'll need to *over*-communicate with engineers on other teams to identify dependencies. Keep in mind, engineers like to talk to other engineers. There's a sort of technical rapport, so you can encourage or coach them to help you."

"In this type of environment, there are likely to be many dependencies. If someone in the far reaches of the company hasn't completed what your team needs, your team will have a ticket, or work to be done, and it may not be actionable."

Additionally, do the best you can to make it visible. Most of the computerized systems like Jira have a feature that allows someone to link tickets together that have a dependency. You must know about it first though."

Avram gave Sully an idea about making dependencies even more visible and would help him coach the team to identify them earlier. He wanted to run it by Fin, the team's Principal Engineer.

Fin is personable, humble, intelligent and organized. With dark brown eyes, he looked at you quizzically, like he was trying to figure out what you are up to. Like he knew better. Almost suspicious. Fin is a big dude with a stocky and athletic build, and short, buzzed hair. He frequently forgot his reading glasses at his desk, and would walk into the conference room, only to turn around, explaining he would be back in a minute.

Sully, having been around the military, had the sense Fin once served. Marine Corps or Army perhaps. Generally soft spoken with an air about him that he is tough as nails, Fin did not share much about his personal life and liked to keep it all about the work at hand.

Sully ventured, "Fin I have an idea I'd like your advice on."

"Go ahead," replied Fin.

"Niko's identified that tickets get stalled, or stopped, during a Sprint. It's mostly because we haven't identified dependencies, either with other teams or within our own backlog."

"I had that same problem last week."

"Well, I'd like to try something and see if we can improve the situation."

Fin cautiously encouraged, "O–k–a–y...what is it?"

"It's simple, really. What if we added a Dependencies text prompt to each Jira ticket. That way it could serve as a reminder before we start working on a ticket. We could do this while we're refining work."

"Can we add a note, like who to contact?" Fin added.

"Sure! And I agree doing this will also help us avoid pulling work into the next Sprint that we can't complete because we need something from someone else."

Sully continued, "If we try it, like an experiment, we can always update or remove it later if for some reason it doesn't work out."

"Sounds low risk, why not?" Fin concluded, wanting to get back to the code he was writing.

Sully returned to the Jira Admin's wishing well again and submitted a request for help.

On his call, he asked the rep, "Could you add three prompts in bold text into the description field of every ticket type except for Bugs for the Cloud team?"

"Sure, what are they?"

A few rows down from the top to leave space for the User Story, please add 'Dev Notes,' 'Documentation,' and 'Dependencies/Risks,' with a few spaces in between.

He could hear the Jira admin typing.

"Okay, refresh your screen and check."

Sully did and requested a few adjustments before they ended the call.

The Dependencies and Risks prompt was to ensure they started to consider both dependencies and risks early in the work ticket creation process, as well as a plan to deal with them.

Sully took a few liberties with the prompts in addition to dependencies. He felt it would be okay with the team.

Because the team was so large, they had already developed the habit of adding developer notes about *how* they were going to approach the solution. Now they had a section specifically for the 'how' notes called "Dev Notes."

Additionally, Sully had overheard a few of the developers complaining that Documentation ought to have been created for a procedure in the past, except it had not. They took their time and attention to fill in the blanks for others. He knew that creating working software was more important than documentation. Still, some documentation was also good to have.

He would ask the team, "What, if any, documentation is required by the end of this work?" He continued, "If it doesn't look like someone has thought about and added notes, I will keep *asking*."

Now, when the team was refining work items, unless these questions had been discussed, answered, and a note made, Sully knew a ticket was not ready to take the last step. Sizing a ticket was the final step before it could be brought into a team Sprint.

If it was not ready or actionable, Sully said, "It's not going into the Sprint."

Sully knew this could be perceived as a controlling, gating, Waterfall-like approach. He also knew that until the team got used to a new way of doing things, it was a necessary evil which would eventually go away. Fixing this one step at a time was in the interest of improving the team's flow of value.

Sully encouraged the developers to reach out to the engineers on the other teams. He sensed they enjoyed it, especially because they were developing a better understanding of how the whole system worked together.

Occasionally, Sully would coordinate work between two teams. After all, if he was going to ask someone to do something, he had better be willing to do it himself. It was especially cool when he got to coordinate work from two teams that happened concurrently, both finishing at the same time between the Cloud team and its Mobile counterpart.

Anyone who has ever worked on large, complex systems has had this same experience. Waiting for someone else's work, or when it shows up, discovering it does not meet the need can be time consuming and frustrating. It requires collaboration. In this case, adding the prompt to Jira was a training tool to help build a new habit.

Now, work could march forward and make progress, instead of getting stalled in the middle of a Sprint, as 80% of the work typically had. Unlike a mechanic that was waiting for parts to fix a car, the Cloud team had all the parts and the tools they needed to complete the work.

A big smile appeared on Sully's face and he chuckled slightly. He was thrilled with the impact the simple improvements were making to the team. By adding the new fields to the tickets, he had not only solved the dependencies problem but also stimulated communication and collaboration among all the engineers on the various teams.

Just as he was mentally giving himself a pat on the back, he overheard someone in the hallway say that code had been lost.

Back to the trenches.

Chapter Five

MORE POWER

"**I**f everyone is moving forward together, then success takes care of itself."

– Henry Ford

Fin caught up with Sully as he was walking toward his cubicle.

"Deployments are messed up."

"Currently we're tracking completed tickets manually on a spreadsheet. One can get missed in tracking completely,"

Sully queried, "What does 'manually' mean?"

"It means we transfer the ticket number and information from one system, Jira, into a spreadsheet. Copy-n-paste."

Sully shook his head, "You're right, that's not efficient; too easy to make a mistake."

"So let me get this straight. We work hard on a solution, write code, validate it, and then it could get lost? I can see how that might happen in the copy-n-paste operation, especially if whoever is doing it gets distracted."

Fin said, "That's correct."

"What if a critical piece is forgotten?" Sully was curious.

"If it's critical, we could've introduced a major bug into the system without even knowing," Fin replied.

"On top of that, we've got to deal with Dominion's numerous moratoriums. Periods when we cannot deploy."

Fin continued, "It makes deploying even more complicated on top of coordinating all the code changes from multiple tickets. Sometimes tickets get lost, then forgotten about. Completed work closes at the end of a Sprint and then kind of, *disappears*." Fin completed his thought.

Sully considered Fin's assessment.

"What are the moratoriums for?" Sully inquired.

"There's several of them. Around weekends, holidays, broadcast blackouts, and financial and other events."

Sully considered the weekend moratoriums to be reasonable because it supported *not* working over the weekends. Good for the team, good for morale.

There was little he could do about the others. After all, it was reasonable that such a large company did not want their whole network to crash for its millions of customers because of some errant bug.

As Sully sank into his office chair, his forehead was crinkled with worry. "That sounds like it could be disastrous, catastrophic event. Let me think about it and get back to you."

Sully did not like what he had heard.

Rightly so, the team was annoyed and often confused about when they could deploy. Sometimes things stacked up because of long moratoriums and it took a lot of effort to unbury. Some were lost.

They waited. They wasted time.

The deployments they were concerned with were on the team's Production servers in the Cloud. 'Prod' is where other teams have access to their backend code so features could be released and exposed to end users.

Sully needed to think about this latest problem. He leaned back in his office chair as he suddenly remembered what Leland, his Lean Six Sigma guru, had said while explaining process 'flow' years earlier.

Leland wore unpleated cotton slacks held up by a brown leather belt that also confined the tails of his tucked in checked or plaid button-up dress shirt. If you had seen him on the street, it would have been impossible to tell what he did for a living by the way he dressed. In his early 40s, he stood about six feet tall and was on the heavier side.

Leland's face had a longer, sandy blond beard that had started to go gray in spots and made his chin look like it was jutting out. He had deep-set blue eyes, with long hair the same color as his beard, pulled back in a ponytail. He spoke and moved with an air of quiet confidence as he was leading his class down an important path.

The training was held in Houston, Texas, and conducted in a similar manner to the Project Management courses Sully had taken. A training session, then back to the office to apply what he had learned, and so on.

"A core tenet of Lean is Value Stream Mapping."

"This is accomplished by mapping all the current process's steps and is often done on a white board or brown paper sheets using Sticky Notes."

"We want to make things 'flow' from one end to the other, from one task to the next in an effortless manner. So, we've got to make the process as efficient as possible."

"Lean tells us to streamline the process by removing as many unnecessary steps and wastes as possible."

A student raised their hand, "You mentioned waste. What are you referring to."

"The sources of Lean's eight wastes are easiest to remember by the acronym *TIMWOODS*. Transportation, Inventory, Motion, Waiting, Overproduction, Overprocessing, Defects, and Skills."

"They are all concerns in industries involving hardware and/or manufacturing," Leland continued.

"What about software?" Sully had asked.

"Well, in software development there are no tangible goods to speak of, so the effects of motion, waiting, overproduction, overprocessing, defects, and skills are still in play."

"For example, code waiting for a review, to be tested, or deployed is an example of wait time, one of the wastes. Defects are another."

"Makes sense," said Sully.

"Software can be a bit tricky," Leland continued, "because it's not physical, unless it's embedded into a physical product."

"How can we overcome that," Sully asked quizzically.

"By using visual tools such as charts, graphs, and boards to display the data, as well as processes. It's even more important with software because it's not tangible!"

"Visual management tools are one of the most important components of Lean and Six Sigma," Leland concluded before he moved on.

Leland's teachings influenced Sully in subtle ways. He reached out to his favorite Jira Admin once again.

"Kazi, I need your advice. I don't want to do anything yet, I only want to know if something is possible to do in Jira."

"Sure, Sully, what's up?" Kazi was only a voice on the video calls.

Sully wondered what Kazi looked like and imagined him with bedhead like the Jira admin he had heard about traveling around the country in his old car.

Sully briefed Kazi on the current situation.

"Is there a way we could have tickets that were closed in a Sprint magically appear on another board, such as a board specifically dedicated for tickets that are ready to deploy for my Cloud team?"

He could hear Kazi clicking away on his keyboard like a maestro playing a piano concerto. Sully still had no idea what Kazi looked like, and he was hopeful he could help him solve this more difficult problem inside Jira.

I checked a few things, and I believe it's possible. I created a quick example. Sending you the link to my share now."

"Got it?"

"I can see it."

Kazi said, "See this ticket in the far-right column, ABC-123? Its Jira status is Closed. When I complete the Sprint, it disappears off the Sprint Board."

"Where'd it go? That's the problem, we need to still track it!" Sully said impatiently.

"Hold on, now watch. Here's a second, Kanban Board I've set up to hold onto it."

Kazi opened the board, and sure enough, ABC-123 was in the far-left column!

"Cool! Let me circle back with the team and come up with a design. Awesome Kazi!" he said as he ended the call.

Within the week, Sully gathered Aishwarya, Fin, George, and Niko for a brief meetup to get their input.

Fin reviewed the deployment disaster problem he had mentioned to Sully recently.

"Sully, did I miss anything?"

"I don't believe you skipped over anything. Manual process, lost tickets, moratoriums. I think you got it."

"Okay," Sully said addressing the group, "I got together with Kazi, one of the Jira Admins, and he worked up a quick example solution, so I know it's possible."

He grabbed a few dry erase markers as he moved to the white board in the ACL conference room, "This is our current Sprint board."

He drew a black square with several columns and walked them through the solution on the white board with a closed ticket moving to a second board.

Then asked, "How many columns do we need on the deployment board?"

They discussed a few ideas and landed upon Completed, Ready to Deploy, and Done. The last one indicated it had been deployed to Production.

Sully got together with Kazi, and they put a full working prototype together for the team to try out so they could see it in action. There were a few items of feedback that were minor in nature.

Two weeks later, Kazi implemented it on the team's live Jira site, and Sully validated it. He certainly did not want to lose any tickets!

After a few weeks of using the new process to deploy, Sully checked in with the team about the new deployment board setup.

"So, how's the new deployment board working for us?"

"We're not going to lose any more tickets," Fin said, showing a rare moment of joy and a slight smile on his face.

Each team member agreed it was a much better system than the one they had before, and a lot easier to use. They would now have more time to write code.

During the next few months, the team managed to earn the trust of Dominion's deployment control group and could now perform automated deployments instead of manually deploying, which was process heavy, time consuming, and approval intensive.

In the future, the team would improve the automated process even further, and could deploy working code *at will*, sometimes even in the middle of a Sprint when another team needed them to. So long as they were steering clear of the moratoriums, it was a tremendous success!

Like a good mechanic working on an old car, Sully knew there was more performance to be had. More horsepower, better brakes and handling, newer systems to protect his investment.

As you know, complex systems have a lot of pieces moving around. How do you keep track of yours? Is it working, or could it be improved?

Fortunately, users typically did not have access to the Cloud team's production code right away because the functionality itself was hidden behind a feature flag.

Only after the Mobile development team had finalized the user interface and received approval from Android and Apple, and the app had gone through a lengthy, rigorous two-week test period, was the feature exposed to users by easily 'flipping' the feature flag.

The improvements the team had made were working well together. The requirements process was more effective, the work understood.

They were getting better at communicating amongst themselves, despite the distance, and they were collaborating more every day with each other as well as the developers on other teams.

So far, the team has overcome some big systemic problems. They were becoming more efficient and effective, and because they were involved in solving the problems, they felt that they owned the resolutions. The changes in Jira helped them to embrace the end-to-end improvements. Repetition was the mother of skill.

Things are starting to get better, Sully thought, *the first layer of the onion.*

These were simple things that had gotten in the way of completing work.

He observed a change in the team's demeanor, too, as if a huge burden had been lifted. The team was happier. Still, Sully suspected there was more to do, the next layer of the onion.

Change was coming just around the corner. A big one. They had no idea.

Chapter Six

MONKEY WRENCH

Part Two

"T he announcement is the easy part; it makes the manager look bold and decisive. Implementation is more difficult..."

– Ron Ashkenas and Rizwan Khan

"I didn't see *that* coming!" Sully screamed. He felt blindsided. There were pieces of glass floating in the air, as if gravity had stopped working. The back of his right thigh hurt. He checked his head for blood, and found none, thankfully. He was rolling down the street on all four wheels.

His 1973 Cutlass had conked out. He had been driving to apply for a part-time job in his first car which he had purchased for $1,500 only a few months before. Like most young men of 17, he had a special connection with his first, despite its flaws.

Sully had entered the intersection cautiously to make a left-hand turn as he waited for the lights to change from green to red. A large six-wheeled box truck with a red cab blocked his view of oncoming traffic. The truck was headed in the opposite direction and had stopped at the light to turn to Sully's right to navigate to the northbound onramp for I-93.

The light turned yellow, then red. Sully waited for three seconds then aimed his pride and joy into the business's driveway. Then out of nowhere...

A fully loaded Z-28 Camaro T-boned Sully's car. It was speeding down the surface street's break-down lane at perhaps 60 miles an hour. The impact shattered the window on the passenger side of Sully's car immediately before his head got there. He was not wearing a seatbelt. He would have flown out of the passenger window if it were not for the armrest, which was in the down position, catching the back of his right thigh.

There was so much force, his car changed direction ninety degrees, and the impact caused the engine to stall. The brakes had lost their power. It was all Sully could do to stop the car eighty yards down the road.

"Shit!" Sully exclaimed.

It was probably a good thing he had not seen the other car coming and had not braced for impact. He patted himself down, checking for anything broken.

Having found none, he collected himself and made his way on foot back to the scene to find out if there was a way he could help. Luckily, the worst injury was a bloody nose earned by someone in the back seat of the Camaro, as well as the driver's bruised ego.

The insurance companies sorted things out. At the deposition, Sully learned the driver and his three passengers were late to work for their swing shift at a local plant. In the end, the insurance companies totaled both cars.

"I guess everything can't be fixed," he told Pops.

As you know, a sudden, unexpected change in direction can make quite an impact. Bad if you are not prepared. Good if you are.

At Dominion's Austin Office, Sully was walking down the hallway to a team meeting and experienced a strange feeling, like a déjà vu or a premonition. He shivered slightly and the hair on his arms started to stand on end. He shook it off and finished his stroll to the meeting, unable to shrug off the nagging feeling that something big was about to happen.

It was early June 2023. As the pandemic faded farther into the past, people were spending the majority of their work week at the office.

Change was in the wind, major change.

A few weeks later, Dominion's Product leaders came to Austin for a dog-and-pony show. All the people in the office gathered in the cafe, since it was the only space large enough to physically host a meeting of 50 or more people. It had a built-in PA system, and a humongous screen on one wall for presenting and projecting the faces of those who joined remotely.

Sully had heard news of the Product leaders' visiting during his team's stand-up earlier that month. Trying to fit in with the Texas culture, they led off with, "We're here to tell *y'all* about our new do-it-yourself home security initiative. The value proposition will be a significant differentiator and will position Dominion as a market leader."

It struck Sully as odd. There was something about someone from Philly saying "y'all" that was weird and not quite right. It did not come off well.

"Product and Engineering leadership have been working diligently over the past few months to make this happen."

"It's imperative to get these five new products and/or features into the end users' hands during the next 12–18 months."

They changed to the next slide with icons for each product or feature. They briefly explained what each one did for the customer, flipping through more slides for each one.

One of the products was for a new, cutting-edge technology that detected movement. One of Sully's teams had been working on it over the past year with a partner company outside of Dominion's reign.

"Motion detection will be offered to customers at no charge to increase interest and engagement in Dominion's do-it-yourself home security system."

"In 18 months, there will be a major broadcast event, and we hope to promote the initiative and these products during the event."

The next slide displayed a timeline. It appeared ambitious to Sully at first glance.

Everybody quickly understood the deadline was immovable.

"This initiative is urgent," they said as if jobs depended upon it, "...and will demand a change in focus for many people."

"We've worked with your development leaders and together, feel like we've determined the best way to organize everybody to meet our goals," they continued.

"Teams will be aligned to the new initiatives and features."

They walked through the new teams and their relationship to each other as they referred to diagrams on the next few slides.

It was clear. Failure was not an option.

Somehow, this new strategy felt different.

Chapter Seven

TIRE IRON

"C oming together is a beginning. Keeping together is progress. Working together is success."

– Andrew Carnegie

"I'm booked solid early in the morning and double-booked for the rest of the days for the next month," George said.

Sully was trying to get 30 minutes of George's time early one morning to get advice on a side project he had been working on.

George continued, "Niko and I both start our days early so we can discuss implementations and coach the offshore folks like Nitin before our team meetings get started."

Sully knew there was still an issue with the team members having enough time to communicate and collaborate.

Things felt rushed during the next refinement meeting. The team was now finalizing ten work items at a time, which was significantly better, however there was still pressure to have more and faster. Sully had to cut conversations short to keep the large group moving forward, irritating Ganesh even more.

"Why don't you send out a list of tickets the day before refinement so the dev's can review them beforehand," Ganesh suggested to Sully.

That helped to a certain degree, but Sully felt like the requests were largely ignored. Nevertheless, discussing requirements was still needed.

Worse, Sully also knew his offshore teammates had additional late-night calls during the week with developers from other teams regarding the dependencies they had been identifying.

To make matters more difficult, they were also up late to help with the team's deployments. It was like pouring gasoline on an already hot fire.

Sully felt bad for his teammates who were offshore, and that the work was interrupting precious family and rest time nearly every day for them.

So, he conducted informal one-on-one surveys with his Austin teammates to see if they could start 60 minutes earlier one or two days a week to ease the burden.

The Austin-based team refused, citing conflicts with family obligations such as driving children to daycare or school.

Sully's one-on-one surveys were a bust.

He was frustrated. They had made progress. Still, it was not enough.

I'm not ready to give up, Sully reassured himself. Somehow, he was able to muster faith that the team's situation could be improved.

Sully was reminded of a conversation he had had in his two-day Scrum class in Boston with Avram.

"How many people are on a Scrum team?" Avram challenged Sully.

He guessed, "Ten?" He had worked with teams that were as large as twenty and directed multiple teams of 20–50 people each.

Avram replied, "The optimal team size is seven, plus or minus two."

"Why is that?" Sully queried.

"Military and scouting patrols are this size, as are other types of teams throughout history."

"A team of only five people has merely ten connections or channels of communication."

"Can you estimate how many channels a team of seven, with only two more people, has?"

"I don't know, fourteen?" Sully replied, doing some simple math in his head.

"Think again," Avram replied, smiling a bit like the Cheshire Cat, "Over twice as many! It's exponential."

"A team of nine has thirty-six, over three times as many channels with four more people than a five-person team."

Sully reflected on some of the larger teams he had worked with. No wonder communication was strained and getting things done was difficult.

"A team that is three times the size of five, has more than ten times the connections!" Avram was clearly excited.

Sully's team was much too large, cumbersome, and inefficient to deal with the massive priority change they were faced with.

The recent refocus on the new initiatives meant widespread change. The composition of Sully's 15-member Cloud team was in the crosshairs. It was too big, and he needed a smaller team that could adapt and be more agile.

Sully had a lot of practice at influencing those above him—those who held higher status and wielded the power to make decisions. He'd been leading through influence for more than ten years, long before anyone gave him a formal title or direct reports. It was harder than most people realized. Without the authority that comes with position, you had to earn every win through trust, data, and strategic timing. You had to understand what kept your leaders up at night, translate technical realities into business language they cared about, and know when to push and when to plant seeds that would grow into their ideas later.

The key to influencing up, Sully had learned, was making your boss look good while solving problems they didn't even know they had yet. It meant bringing solutions, not complaints. It meant understanding the political landscape two levels above you and framing your proposals in terms of their priorities, not yours. Most importantly, it meant building credibility through consistent delivery—because when you had no formal power, your track record was your only currency.

The first change included splitting off eight of the offshore engineers into their own team with their own Engineering Manager. Sully was somehow both sad and grateful at the same time that Dominion had split them off.

Sully was curious to know if this was a result of a past conversation he had had with Carlos about the team's size. He thought Carlos had his hand in the pie-making process, regardless.

Sully's manager, Carlos, was the Director of Software Engineering. Carlos was from Austin and had a degree in Engineering from Texas A&M. He managed the two Cloud development teams Sully worked with, was experienced in both mobile app and Cloud software development and had been a people leader for seven years. He was an advocate for Agile and was pretty good at controlling his impulse to chime in on engineering decisions as a former developer himself.

Carlos grew up in Austin's indie music scene. He played bass guitar and had recorded a few albums with an emo band back in the 80's that achieved moderate success. He was in his late 40's, tall and lanky, like most bass guitar players Sully knew. He wore loose-fitting t-shirts and jeans, with sneakers and stylish reading glasses. His slim face was topped with short black hair tinged with grey, as was his two-day-old unshaven beard.

Splitting the offshore teammates into their own team was not the only change.

The Cloud team's Software Engineering Manager, Ganesh, also changed seats.

Would the new manager be an improvement? Sully decided to keep an open mind.

The team's new software engineering manager was Jack.

He also had responsibility to write requirements or user stories for the team.

Jack was tall, like most of the engineering managers in the Austin office. He was in his late 30's-early 40's, with a thick stubble beard and a head full of hair, cut short. His appearance reflected his active lifestyle. He wore patterned, casual, button-down short-sleeved shirts and jeans, both a little baggy since he had been losing weight.

Sully liked Jack. Early on, Jack established a collaborative, confident work vibe with him. Then again, Jack occasionally had some quirky reactions to things. Sully quickly found out that Jack preferred that Sully run new ideas or proposed changes by him before bringing them to the team. Sully preferred to be open with all the people on the team, getting their input and ideas on changes.

Jack also reported to Carlos, making Sully and Jack peers as he had been with Ganesh.

Jack embraced his new responsibilities as the team's manager and its Product Owner with vigor. He kept the product backlog of work items (requirements) clean and in priority order by working with the team.

Not once did he show signs of inner conflict the way Ganesh had. It was like he had been doing it all his life.

Ganesh returned to the role he once relished and better suited his personality, working remotely with other teams as a Principal Software Engineer.

A third change was with team personnel. Two team members were laid off, and two new developers joined Aishwarya, Fin and Niko on the team.

The team's struggles with communicating and collaborating, the odd hours, and meetings that were too short, eased significantly. Sully saw other benefits as well.

Now there was no rush to refine work, no odd or late-night hours because the team was co-located.

The team now had only seven members, including Jack and Sully, and only twenty-one channels of communication instead of over a hundred.

There was also now an opportunity to collaborate face-to-face, since every team member was based in Austin.

The smaller team would also give Sully the fuel he needed to make the team's Scrum meetings more efficient, effective, and valuable.

Often, when one problem is fixed, another raises its head.

Pivoting to the new product strategy direction seemed daunting.

The team was dealing with layoffs, changing team-mates, and a new manager, and Sully was still play-ing Whack-a-Mole, trying to address countless prob-lems.

The management changes and spinning off the off-shore team had given Sully the breathing room he needed. Now he could create a strategic plan to form the team into a cohesive, high performing unit that could effectively meet the new company objectives despite the tight deadline.

Remember a time when you had a flat tire? Even though it felt a little dangerous because you had to swap out a wheel on the side of the road, you knew what to do to solve the problem, and you had the tools to do it.

Different story if the road was covered by a bucket of nails that dislodged itself from a carpenter's truck, sprinkling sharp metal objects all over the road. Mul-tiple flats would be a more complex problem altogeth-er, as you could imagine!

At Dominion, the cloud team's communication and personnel issues had been resolved, but their atten-tion now turned to a new, larger challenge. The group had to transform as a new team and get oriented toward the new priorities.

It would take time and patience for the new group to become a team together. Let the healing begin.

Chapter Eight

ALIGNMENT

"The best teamwork comes from those who are working independently toward one goal in unison."

– James Cash Penney

"Do you have a few minutes?" Sully inquired as he interrupted Carlos in his office cubicle. The cubicle was like all the others, with one special feature, it was up against an outer window. All of the more senior leaders had the same setup. Carlos had a pile of small, older electronic home security devices on half his desk.

Sully perked up, "For us to have a fighting chance, we need to align the teams' goals to the new strategy,"

"The timelines are going to be incredibly tight, and it appears that missing the deadline is not an option." He was feeling the pressure.

"I have a suggestion."

"What is it?" Carlos questioned.

"I'd like to help the teams develop a Rally Cry."

"What's that?"

"It's a technique to clearly align team goals to strategy. I learned about it from the business leadership book called, '*Silos, Politics, and Turf Wars*' by Patrick Lencioni."

Sully added, "The book tells a story and illustrates how to develop a 'Thematic Goal 'with supporting objectives."

"After helping a few teams go through the exercise in the past, I've found the term *Rally Cry* to be more user friendly."

"It's an enormously powerful way to unite a team and drive them forward, especially when something critical is on the line. In our case, the deadline."

"The exercise takes a little bit of time, up to several hours."

"The important thing is that *the team* creates its Rally Cry and owns it together. They 'rally' around it."

"I'm not sure I understand," said Carlos. "I'd like to learn more."

Sully replied, "I can lend you the book. It's a quick read. I'll bring it in tomorrow."

"Okay, find a team that's willing to give it a try and we'll see how it goes," Carlos was already planning, "If we end up doing this for all the teams in the division, you'll need to train someone so they can help you."

Sully created a presentation and called a meeting in the ACL conference room with a team that was focused on improving mobile developer processes and was willing to try the new idea first.

He explained, "Creating a Rally Cry enables a team to pinpoint where it needs to focus, provides clarity, and sets us up for success."

Sully continued, "It minimizes confusion and politics while simplifying decision making for teams and people at all levels."

Sully clarified, "A Rally Cry is a meaningful, qualitative, single statement that clarifies the team's goal and is easily remembered. We will also need to look beyond our team, group, and division, and discover our team's part in the larger picture."

He continued, "It's supported by a few key objectives to make it happen, like pillars that support a roof."

"If done well, it will be easy to remember and will stir your emotions. It will mean something to each of you."

To clarify even further, he added, "A Rally Cry is not meant to take the place of Dominion's mission; its intent is to connect strategy to a team's short-term goals. It is temporary, lasting only for a clearly defined timeframe, in our case, the next 12 – 18 months."

Sully discussed some ways a Rally Cry helps the team. One specifically stood out, "Each teammate can now refer to the Rally Cry to determine if a task is in alignment with the team's goal and quickly decide what action to take."

"It's especially useful when getting requests from another team that are out of the blue, that could cause a distraction. You then could politely decline and avoid going down a rabbit hole."

To help the team craft their Rally Cry, Sully asked a series of questions and added key words they said onto the whiteboard. Some were erased, more added. They started to cobble a single statement together. As the team discussed it, their Rally Cry started to come into focus.

> *"Make the lives of mobile developers easier by improving the tools they use to enable fast development and deployment."*

"Not bad!" Sully offered some feedback.

"It contains who, what, and why. The where, when, and how are implied."

The primary objectives were related to the tools for building and deploying mobile app code, and delivering customer value, with an emphasis on communicating and collaborating across multiple mobile development teams.

He had learned about the struggles the app developers were having from one of the teams he was working with. Getting builds to merge into the code base was often painful, with a lot of waiting. There were fourteen other mobile app teams that had the same experience. Sully was eager to hear about the progress the first Rally Cry team had made, and the impact they had on his own mobile developers.

Sully led this exercise for two leadership groups in his division and his own teams, including the Cloud team. The Scrum Master he trained was successful in developing Rally Cries with four other teams.

Sully's reconfigured Cloud team appeared to be jelling quickly. They had a renewed focus on the work and were making great strides toward their goals early on. It was working.

The Rally Cry focused and aligned objectives with team goals for the company's near-term strategy for the big initiative. It was making things happen.

"I've never seen a Rally Cry work like *this* before," he told Carlos, "The teams are coming together quickly!"

Either Sully was getting better at it, or there really was something special about the people he worked with. Maybe both.

Plus, good things can come from organizational changes,

similar to when a mechanic aligns the wheels of a car using a special computerized rack and factory specifications.

The goal of the operation is to ensure the vehicle drives straight and does not wear out the tires prematurely. Unchecked, poor alignment and uneven tire wear could eventually cause an accident.

Chapter Nine

TRICKY DIAGNOSIS

Part Three

"**P**ure logical thinking cannot yield us any knowledge of the empirical world; all knowledge of reality starts from experience and ends in it."

– Albert Einstein

It was 10:00 am on a Friday the weather was overcast with big dark clouds as a new black Chevy Suburban pulled into the service drive.

The clouds looked like they were going to unleash a downpour at any minute. It was a good thing she parked under the overhang.

The driver climbed down from the cabin and made her way through the glass door. She was dressed in a business-like, navy-blue blazer with two silver buttons over a delicate white blouse, gray slacks, and sensible black shoes with low heels.

Her hair was pulled back, and she did not appear to be wearing much makeup, if any. She carried herself with an air of authority.

As she approached Keith, who was behind the dealership's service desk, propped on a tall shop stool, he thought she looked like an agent of some sort.

"My car makes this funny noise and loses power. I need you to fix it," she said.

Keith started making some notes, typing on his computer.

"What does the noise sound like?"

"I hear a faint 'whirrr' sound," she tried to imitate it, then continued, "and then it hesitates for a minute."

"Where is the noise coming from?"

"Sounds like it's coming from the dashboard near the windshield," she replied.

"You mentioned it *hesitates*. What do you mean?"

"Well, I step on the gas, trying to accelerate, except it doesn't respond."

"So, it seems like it loses power from the engine."

"Yes."

He asked, "When does it happen?"

Keith imagined he was a detective with all the questions. It was part of his job however, to gather information so technicians could diagnose the problem correctly. Tricky problems required more attention and more questions.

"I don't know, when I'm trying to accelerate."

"All the time?"

"No, she said, "What do you mean by *when does it happen?*"

"You know, time of day, how fast are you going, how long have you been driving. That sort of thing."

"Let me think for a minute." *Long pause.*

"I believe it's mostly when I've been driving it for some time. I do a lot of stop-and-go driving. If it's cold out and I'm parked, I keep the engine and heater running to stay warm."

Keith visualized her on a stakeout outside of some criminal's house, parked in the shadows a short distance down the street on a dark, drizzly night with halos circling the streetlamps overhead.

"I'm afraid I'm going to get stuck in the middle of an intersection and someone will run into me. I only had it for a few months. This kind of thing shouldn't happen to a new vehicle, right?"

"That's correct," Keith responded with precision, "How long have you been driving it this morning?"

"I've been running errands for an hour or so, and it happened again right before I came upon your dealership."

"What's your name, address, and phone, Miss? I'll need it for the repair order."

She reluctantly complied. She did not like giving out personal information.

"Miss Jackson, would it be okay if I had a technician go for a test drive with you, see if you can reproduce it?"

"Sure, I guess, how long will this take?"

"Depends on how quickly it happens. Once it does, it could be a few minutes, a few hours, or a few days after we've determined what it'll take to fix it."

"I'll be right back," Keith said as he walked through the door into the shop.

She could see him through the wired safety glass in the top half of the door as he approached one of the mechanics.

Keith returned and instructed, "Tom will meet you out at the car. You'll drive."

She was able to duplicate the issues twice within a couple of blocks and after returning to the service drive with her Suburban, she hopped out of the driver's seat.

Tom pulled her Suburban into his service bay, opened the hood, and pulled out a gauge or two. After he had run a few quick tests he replaced a length of vacuum hose, took it for a test drive, and returned the vehicle to the dealership's service driveway, aimed toward the street.

Keith indicated, "You are all set. There was a pinhole in a vacuum line we replaced."

"Thank you for handling this quickly!" she said and shook his hand over the counter, revealing a badge affixed to her belt on one side and a bulge shaped like a handgun on the other.

A great mechanic first diagnoses a problem, then selects the correct tools and parts to make the repair before they test it. If the problem is fixed, great!

However, if it is not, they need to start all over again, spending their own, non-billable time. Diagnosis is emphasized to avoid making a mistake, like the old 'measure twice, cut once' rule.

The Cloud team had already taken steps in the right direction. They had made significant reductions in work delays and task switching. They were communicating and collaborating with each other and developers in other teams. They had recently developed a laser-like focus, due to the fact they were a much smaller team now. The Cloud team was starting to perform even better than before.

Yet, there were still times when the work that was committed was not completed on time. The question was why.

Leaders want their teams to provide customer value predictably and with high quality, all while being highly productive and delivering a return on investment.

Unfortunately, in this situation, something was off. Whatever it was, it kept the team from achieving a steady flow of value to its customers.

Could the problem be within the team? Were legacy practices, best practices, or processes getting in the way? Was planning effective? What was going on inside the two-week iteration?

There was a lot on the line. Sully was missing something.

Chapter Ten

THE MAP

"I n preparing for battle I have always found that plans are useless, but planning is indispensable."

– Dwight D. Eisenhower

Sully had been laser focused on the problems *outside* the team that stalled development and kept them from completing work. They were big systematic issues and resolving one often led to the discovery of another. They each had been handled in turn.

Now, it's time to focus on the team's process, Sully thought.

The devil was always in the details.

Sully considered the planning process. Each team member and Jack, acting as the Product Owner, defined a Sprint Goal, and selected work tickets to include in the Sprint.

Frequently, Jack asked a developer if they could do 'this one extra ticket' during planning sessions, just before kicking off the new Sprint.

A common response from an accommodating developer was, "Sure, I can do that," and the extra ticket was pulled into the Sprint whether or not it supported the Sprint goal.

Two weeks later when the Sprint ended, there were unfinished work items. Sometimes, the extra tickets had been completed while the item that supported the Sprint goal had not.

Occasionally they would exercise better judgement. If an added ticket was larger, they would pull another out to compensate. Frequently, that was not the case.

Each team member estimated what they thought they could complete in the two-week period, often overestimating their capacity, Sully realized.

In addition, *agreeing to an extra task is likely a subconscious or knee-jerk response to Jack, their manager.*

He became acutely aware of things that were happening after planning had been completed, and the Sprint had already started. There were distractions and scheduling conflicts, and there was overcommitment.

Team members would say, "It's taking longer than I thought because I got pulled into a big technology discussion."

"I forgot about a two-day class."

"We have *Innovation Week* next week, and I decided to participate only a few hours ago!"

"I committed to too many tickets."

These excuses and more caused work that was committed to during planning to be incomplete by the end of the iteration. Then the incomplete work would carry over into the next Sprint. They overreacted and committed to a lot less new work, overestimating what it would take for the older tickets to cross the line.

It was feast or famine.

To Sully, the situation felt like driving on 'whoop-de-do's,' a road that looked like a roller coaster with hills and troughs that would make his stomach queasy. He was concerned the team felt the same way.

Measuring the team's velocity alone was not going to cut it. Besides, velocity by itself is known to be misinterpreted often and can be unreliable. Sully needed a better tool to help sort it out.

Steve approached Sully in the Austin office at his cube. He was visiting for a few days, and motioned toward ACL, which was empty and close to Sully's cube, indicating he wanted Sully to join him for an impromptu meeting.

Steve is an engineering leader that took an interest in Sully. He lived in San Diego, worked remotely, and considered himself a 'Master of Sheets,' or spreadsheets.

Steve was a few inches shorter than Carlos and Sully, and slim. He dressed in slacks or jeans, with a patterned dress shirt on top. He too had a mix of gray in his scruffy dark beard, short salt and pepper hair, and wore conservative glasses. He constantly had a smile on his face and a genuine laugh ready at any moment.

Steve was adept at turning potentially bad conflicts into action in such a way that afterward, those involved felt positive and energized.

"Check this out," Steve opened a file, "I've been working on a better way to estimate what we could handle, scope wise, when we do quarterly planning."

"This estimates our group's capacity so we can compare estimated t-shirt sizes."

"We also try to take into account paid-time-off, company events, and other factors so we don't commit to too much work."

Sully's mind was racing, especially because he thought he could use the same spreadsheet, with a few improvements, for the Cloud team's Sprint planning. It was definitely what he was looking for.

"Could you send me a copy, Steve?"

It was exactly the tool Sully needed. Using Steve's spreadsheet as a starting place, Sully added another tab for tracking the results of each Sprint with allowances for time away as Steve had done.

Sully leaned forward in his desk chair, rubbing his temple with a forefinger, deep in thought, evaluating his creation wholistically.

We still need something to account for the tickets that carry over. What about other risks, the uncertainty that things will go better than planned as well as the uncertainty when they don't.

He added the ability to account for work remaining that carried into the next Sprint. He also added an easy method to account for uncertainty, based on experience. It was not a highly complex or scientific method. It was merely a great reminder to account for risk, and he liked the elegance of its simplicity.

Sully began referring to the new tool as the 'Crystal Ball.'

Another built-in feature of the Crystal Ball accounted for average non-productive time, such as administrative overhead and meetings. Lead engineers tended to spend more time meeting with others than their teammates.

Sully also linked the two spreadsheets in the workbook, so actual Sprint data fed the quarterly planning estimates and improved its accuracy.

He started using the Crystal Ball with his teams immediately.

It was a little clunky to use because it was a spreadsheet, however because Sully had developed it, he knew its ins and outs.

Before Sprint planning, Sully approached Jack in his cubical. Jack was looking at his monitors intensely, as though he was evaluating a tricky problem, and was listening to something through his headphones, and removed them as Sully approached.

Glad he was not interrupting a meeting, Sully said, "I feel the developers consistently overestimate their capacity for each Sprint, maybe with the exception of Niko."

"I've developed a new tool that estimates how much work the team and each team member ought to take on in the next Sprint. It's based on something Steve has been developing for quarterly planning.

"I believe we can use it to help the team to take on the right amount of work, not too much, not too little."

"Then, with a little data entry, it accounts for each person's vacations and company holidays. It even accounts for events like Innovation Week and the amount of work remaining on a carry-over ticket and adjusts the estimate accordingly."

"You as the PO and the team still determine the Sprint goal and what tickets are included in the Sprint. The Crystal Ball provides estimates to use as a guide in planning."

"Sounds good," Jack said less than enthusiastically, as if he did not understand he had a problem that needed fixing.

On the other hand, if Steve was the source, it couldn't be all bad.

"Based on these estimates, our target is 45 new points of work for the iteration starting next week."

"So, what do you want me to do?"

"As the Product Owner, could you prioritize the product backlog's tickets before planning so that the most important

ones for the next Sprint are clearly at the top, plus some?"

"Sure, I guess."

"It will help to shorten the Sprint planning meeting," Sully said, knowing full well that Jack was overwhelmed by meeting after meeting, and would appreciate the break.

After a time, the seven-person team became so good at preparing for the Sprint planning meetings 'offline,' that they were able to close the previous Sprint and kick off the next, one in a mere 15 minutes instead of one hour!

Sully continued, "And because we'll need up-to-the-minute estimates for the work remaining on carry-overs, I'll need to get that info at the beginning of planning and then communicate how much work each team member can handle. Is that okay?"

"Let's give it a try and see what happens," Jack replied.

It seemed as if Jack had embraced experimenting.

During next week's planning session, Sully briefly explained the tool, its data, and how it worked to the team.

Things did not go exactly as Sully had hoped. Jack and the team kept trying to include too much work.

Sully reminded them of the estimates and with a little negotiating amongst the team, the improvement that was made was not enough.

It was a start. Sully knew it would take the team some getting used to until they had faith in what the Crystal Ball provided.

Over the next few Sprints, the team embraced the predictions, once they realized it would help them be better at planning and avoid being over-committed.

A few weeks later, Sully shared the combined tool with Steve during his one-on-one meet up online.

"Check *this* out!" Sully said excitedly.

He briefly walked Steve through the flow of data, the calculation logic, and how it all rolled up to a quarterly estimate, including inputs for time away.

Steve complimented Sully, "This is awesome!" stifling a 'dude,' "Let's use your version to pre-plan your teams' commitments for the next quarter!"

Sully agreed, and after a few quarters wondered if someone might have already automated the process. Spreadsheet files are so late 20th century. Surely someone had.

The Crystal Ball was instrumental at controlling the amount of work-to-do going into each Sprint. The roller coaster effect was going away, things were becoming smoother, and even more work was getting completed. In fact, Sully felt that he could see the proverbial light at the end of the tunnel.

For a well-conceived road trip, a good driver plans it out using a map that clearly shows a destination and the most direct way to arrive on time. It was not too long ago that we all used large-scale folding maps we had picked up from the Automobile Association, or a Thomas Guide which contained detailed maps of city streets. At the time, these were cutting edge, and the best thing available.

Do you remember those?

Today, we have Maps and Waze to assist us when plotting a course across town or from coast to coast. Plus, both phone apps can direct us to alternate routes in real time, to avoid traffic jams. No unfolding a map or page flipping.

Even though there had been marked improvement with the new planning based on real capacity, there was still something preventing flow.

Sully had heard a leadership advisor once say, "Don't sweat the small stuff."

Then again, Sully knew that sometimes, small things matter.

Chapter Eleven

DASHBOARD

A useful measure is both accurate (in that it measures what it says it measures) and aligned with your goals. Don't measure anything unless the data helps you make a better decision or change your actions."

– Seth Godin

Imagine for a moment if your car had no gauges and no indicator lights on its dashboard. You would have no idea about how fast you were going or the health of the engine.

You would also not have any idea as to what was causing that unexpected rumble or noise or what could be happening when you had pressed on the gas or brakes, and nothing happened.

You would have to shut the car off and call for help. After the tow truck appeared, you'd be off to the mechanic, your day interrupted with no indication about what you were in for.

The same occurred to Sully in Dominion's development environment.

Now that the roadblocks outside the team had been addressed, the developers could make progress on their work items.

Unfortunately, something was still causing tickets to pile up much like a rush hour traffic jam. It happened late in a Sprint before it closed. Many were not getting completed.

Perhaps there were process issues within the team.

Solve problems, others surface.

It was not about making the team go faster. It was about being able to steer and be more agile, at a stable and effective pace.

About six months ago, a coworker, Elli, approached Sully as he was walking down the hallway.

Elli had a kind, round face with a fair complexion. Her hair was straight and dyed a brilliant color and she wore colorful glasses. In her early 30's, she spoke with a midwestern twang and was fluent in code-speak. She was also a member of the Cloud team Sully had been working with.

"You look sad today, Sully."

Sully's face looked as though he'd just learned his dog had died.

"You're the second person that's made that comment today. Do you have a minute?"

Sully motioned for Elli to join him in a conference room they were standing next to.

Once inside, Sully remained standing, resting a hand on the back of the tall black conference chair, and said, "I'm frustrated. I've been here a while and love working with the people."

Elli encouraged him to go on, "Yeah…"

"It seems like a constant battle, there's so much to do, and I feel like we're so far away from achieving a steady flow in each Sprint," he continued.

"Sometimes it's too much to consider, and I question my future here."

"I know how you feel, Sully. When I first started at Dominion, I felt like I didn't know anything. It was my first real job out of school, and I was new in town."

"But my bills were getting paid, and I focused on learning the system and learning the new technologies we'd been digging into," she continued.

"Now I'm in a leadership program for engineers and have my sights on becoming an E3 on my way to Principal Engineer."

"How did you turn things around?" Sully inquired.

"I stuck with it and eventually I made progress, and a plan emerged. I only had to be patient, wait it out, and keep moving forward!"

Sully exclaimed, "Wow! That's great advice. I *believe* we've made progress. I get overwhelmed sometimes, and it gets me down."

"I wasn't trying to give advice necessarily, merely share my experience," Elli replied.

"You're right Sully, I'm definitely aware of the improvements you've made, and they have directly impacted how I do my job. Before you got here, I spent most of my time fighting the system. Now, I look forward to coming into work because I can focus on doing what I love – – writing code to solve engineering problems. I owe that to you."

Sully replied, attempting to be punny, "I feel a *megabyte* better. Thanks for the pep talk Elli."

She shook her head, like she had heard the worst dad joke of all time, as they left the conference room to carry on with their day.

Sully was hungry for a small set of metrics, like a dashboard on a high-performance car, except for the Cloud team.

Years ago, he had heard a speaker at a seminar quote Mark Twain, "Success is the result of good judgement. Good judgement is the result of experience. Experience is the result of poor judgement."

It struck a chord with Sully for some reason and that was why now he made it a habit to learn from other's experiences as a first step, a lesson imprinted on him as a teenager when he had busted his knuckles on the family's Malibu.

Both Avram and Leland had coached him on the importance of visualizing information for a team and making it available for all to see. It was a valuable form of feedback. Leland had also taught Sully about mapping the stream of value.

Sully reclined in his cube's desk chair with his hands clasped behind his head and stared out the window at the trees on the hill outside the office. He recalled a conversation from the third Lean Six class Leland taught many moons ago on metrics and using Minitab.

"Alright, a lot of organizations go crazy with metrics. Each manager wants their own set of a dozen key factors to measure. Unfortunately, a problem arises when the metrics are unique to the manager."

"When multiple managers have multiple metrics to track, not only is it a lot more work to put systems in place, but the dashboards for leadership also now contain hundreds of metrics. The display is crowded and virtually unusable."

Leland pulled up an example of a dashboard with over 100 metrics on it on the screen at the front of the classroom. It was teeming with information and difficult to read. Sully's classmates squinted and leaned forward, attempting to decipher it. After about 10 seconds, one student swiped his hand in the air like he had given up, leaned back in his chair, and rubbed his eyes as if they hurt.

Sully spoke up, "I've seen this same thing in our own organization. An executive had their own set, and together with their six manager's metrics, the dashboard contained something like sixty metrics, and each manager was fighting to have theirs at the top."

"That sounds like a mess," replied Leland, continuing, "With the terabytes of data available to us today on all kinds of variables, it's easy to go overboard."

"So, it's important to be *especially* intentional when selecting metrics. Choose a handful of meaningful ones that will support the organizations strategy and many teams' goals."

"How do we do that," Sully asked, "...especially across multiple managers?"

"Carefully." *Pauses and takes a breath for dramatic effect.* "It requires a lot of collaboration and communication, and may take some time, especially when there are many factors involved. The discussion could generate some conflict and controversy."

"It's also important to use good data practices and let the data tell the story honestly. If the statistics are manipulated to provide a desired result, it will damage your credibility. We'll cover this as our next topic"

"The important thing is that you end up with a small set, no more than half a dozen, that can serve as many people's needs as possible."

"Definitely make sure they are visible. If it isn't measured and communicated, it didn't happen." Leland concluded.

Sully also learned about good data and statistical practices, such as, a larger sample size was always better, and that when reporting metrics, the supporting data must be at least another level below the metric itself.

Embracing Leland's sage advice, Sully set out to research a new scorecard. He remembered his friend Sean enthusiastically going on about something called a 'Balanced Scorecard,' from about 10 years ago, and how Sean told him he had created one for useability. Sully needed something like that to monitor the Cloud team's processes.

He revisited what a Balanced Scorecard was and how it was used to evaluate an organization's performance. The concept had originally been defined by Kaplan and Norton in Feb 1992's version of the Harvard Business Review.

A Balanced Scorecard included four elements: Customer (satisfaction), Financial Health, Internal Processes (operational efficiency), and Learning and Growth (organizational health). These essential elements balanced each other out.

The idea was to monitor the others when a change was made to improve the performance of one. For instance, if a change was made to improve profits, they did not want to see customer satisfaction, the internal process, or organization health suffer.

Sully also learned about a Balanced Scorecard specifically designed for Agile teams during a remote lean coffee session that was hosted by a notable Agile consultancy out of Atlanta, Georgia. In their version, all the reports also related to one another and balanced each other out.

The facilitator indicated, "Each level in a company would have a different Balanced Scorecard treatment. At the team level, they are focused on delivering valuable quality software and functionality to customers, predictably, on a cadence."

"Mid-level management is focused on predictability of value delivery, cost, and progress to goal using metrics around the key results for initiatives," they continued.

"Executives are focused on where they stand in regard to achieving their strategic initiatives and plans, including profitability."

Unfortunately, Sully could not get the consultancy to share an example for a team scorecard, despite his bird–dogging efforts. Regardless, he was not going to let that slow him down. This was the visualization he was after.

He needed a Balanced Scorecard that promoted adaptability. The elements would be related to requirements, predictability, performance, and product quality.

Chapter Twelve

GUAGES

"**D**ata visualization is the language of decision making. Good charts effectively convey information. Great charts enable, inform, and improve decision making."

– Dante Vitagliano

Sully dove headlong into the project.

First up was to see if it was even feasible.

The three teams Sully was working with at the time were using Jira, and he could get his hands on the data. Check.

Jira had a plug-in that was a business intelligence (BI) tool or application for reporting. It produced simple metric/reports for visualizing Jira's data *and* had the ability to create custom reports. Check, check.

The reports could be published on a dashboard in Jira and the team had access. Check, check, check.

Sully identified five reports that he felt fit together and could provide a *balance* at the team level.

They were Predictability Ratio, Readiness Ratio, two for Productivity, and one for Product Quality.

For now, he would assess the team's health informally through observation, because Sully did not have access to Dominion's *employee-based* Net Provider Score (eNPS) survey results.

For customer analytics, the mobile app collected real-time usage data on its security features. Dominion also conducted quarterly *customer-based* Net Promoter Score (NPS) surveys,

Next, Sully conceived a plan of action, which was to learn the BI tool and how to create custom reports so he could develop the reports he had designed in the background while his team was getting used to the new requirements and deployment processes. He could work on his new side hustle in his extra work time, an hour or two here or as time allowed.

He had some difficulty getting the data represented correctly in the metrics, due to some quirks inherent in the tool he was using. Sully relied on the help of the engineers at the BI company located in Latvia, which is eight hours ahead of Austin.

The time difference presented its own set of challenges and reminded Sully of trying to collaborate with the people on the original offshore team. In any case, the people at the BI company were helpful and patient with Sully.

One particularly difficult challenge was calculating the work that was completed, which was a subset of work committed two weeks earlier and did not include work that had been completed outside the context of work committed to at the start of the iteration. There was a lot of back-n-forth, although in the end, they nailed it. This one report took six months to get right.

Sully called a special meeting with the Cloud team, after he had completed the reports' development, to review the dashboard, metrics, and their new reports. The team gathered in the ACL conference room.

"With extensive research and your help, I've created five reports for our dashboard to help us monitor and keep an eye out for additional improvements we could make. These reports makeup our Adaptability Scorecard." He said, drawing air quotes.

"The five reports in an Adaptability Scorecard are for executives, development leaders, and self-improving teams like us."

"All the reports on the dashboard show near real-time data from our project in Jira."

Sully pulled up his presentation with pictures of his designs and projected it onto the screen.

"I have personally validated the data coming across is accurate and calculated in the reports, as designed."

That statement gained a lot of respect from the developers based on the positive head nods around the room.

"Generally, Green is good, Red is bad. Blue has been used selectively in part for accessibility for anybody who is colorblind," he elaborated.

Moving on, Sully leaned in.

"The first two reports are like two of the gauges on your car's dashboard, similar to the speedometer or tachometer, and the second like the gas gauge."

"Our first one is the Predictability Ratio/Activity report. It provides us with a key metric for how effective we are in creating value as it flows through the system. It also provides key information for quarterly and longer-term planning that development leaders and executives have a vested interest in."

"This report shows the primary metric and so much more. It displays other, important activity that could influence the ratio. The report's objective is to help development teams understand how well we're planning and executing short iterations and motivates us to investigate potential problems in the system that need to be improved."

"The Predictability Ratio metric determines how much work the team could complete in a two-week Sprint *predictably,*" Sully said, moving on.

"When we have good data to base decisions on and can observe whether or not improvements point us in a better direction, I believe we ought to use it."

"Now look how far we've come over the past seven Sprints!" Sully pointed to the chart.

"Our Predictability Ratio is trending up, which is great!"

"How well were we doing when I joined?" Sully asked rhetorically.

"This team was *not* predictable *or* productive at all back when we had fifteen engineers and all kinds of roadblocks," George stated, "It was nearly impossible to make any progress. Things are much better now."

The progress they had made was obvious, and the team was stabilizing, even though Sully knew there was more to improve.

"The Predictability Ratio compares what we committed to at the beginning of the Sprint, to what was actually completed by the end of the Sprint." *Long pause.*

He stopped to check for puzzled looks. Either they understood or flat-out did not get it. It was important they understood what he had said, and he was expecting questions.

After what seemed like a few minutes, but was not more than 30 seconds, Aishwarya spoke up.

"What happens when a bug ticket is submitted and completed during a Sprint, yet it's not actually pulled into the Sprint?"

Sully moved to the whiteboard in the conference room and created about 10 blue dots inside a circle with a dry erase marker.

"As an example, imagine these dots represent the work we committed to at the start of the Sprint."

He picked up a green marker and circled only eight of the ten dots, indicating, "These eight are the ones completed."

Looking at Aishwarya, "Your bug," he creates another dot outside either circle using a red marker, then continues, "This work isn't counted because it was not committed to in Sprint planning."

"It's not a bad thing to fix a bug in this manner, only that it's not accounted for in the Predictability Ratio's calculation."

Checking, he continued, "Other ticket types completed outside the context of a Sprint also work the same way. Unfortunately, if a lot of work is being done outside the Sprint, it's an issue."

Niko asked, "Why is that a problem?"

"It could indicate there are *distractions* keeping us from making our Sprint goal. If there are a lot of them, that's not good."

"Occasionally, it will happen though," he said with emphasis, "...and that is okay. We want to reflect on what *actually* happens to give us an opportunity to identify more improvements."

"Why do we want to reflect what happened?" Fin inquired.

Sully continued, "If there's too much traffic with tickets coming into or out of a Sprint, it could indicate some other process may need to be improved, like in Niko's situation a number of Sprints ago."

Niko shared his 'cart before the horse' story. You remember it was about a ticket that could not be completed because it was dependent upon another ticket that was in the product backlog, and the dependency had not been identified.

Sully followed Niko, "The ticket was pulled into the Sprint before it was closed."

"This report can help us identify that same kind of problem," Sully said.

"There's a lot of value we get from this report."

"First, it will help us understand how skilled we are at planning Sprints, developing a cadence, and improving outcomes."

They followed along, so Sully continued, "It tells us if too much work was planned for a Sprint, which is a common problem. It will also tell us if there is too little, as well as show work being pulled in or out while the Sprint is in progress."

"The Predictability Ratio will help predict our flow of outcomes, or customer value that we are delivering to leaders and executives, and ultimately customers. It will also help us improve our quarterly planning, so we don't commit to too much work or, conversely, too little. People will know what to expect."

This drew the attention of the team. Sully could see a look of concern on a few faces and had a pretty good idea as to why and stepped in to address it.

"Your managers have agreed *not* to use this data to evaluate individual performance, and they know *not* to compare teams based on it."

"Understanding the data informs us how we could use it more responsibly."

He continued, "The data is estimate–based and has some level of variability. Besides, each team will size their work differently."

He did not want the team to dwell on this issue too long, so Sully got up from his chair and moved to the screen. It was now displaying the live version of the Cloud team's Predictability Ratio chart.

"This solid line here," Sully pointed, "…is the Pre-dictability Ratio."

"See how the line has peaks and valleys. Some of those are due to tickets carrying over into the next Sprint."

"Some are a result of tickets coming to a standstill because we're waiting on someone outside our team to do something. They take more time to complete"

Sully intentionally avoided calling anyone out. From what he observed so far, it was often a cross–team issue and was no fault of the members of his team.

"Our goal is to smooth that solid line out and get our trend to be consistent and high."

"What do you mean by high," Jack asked.

"Better than 80%," replied Sully, "That is, given our situation with deployments, and that features are hidden behind a feature flag until they're ready for release. The chain of custody is long."

"If we were delivering working code to end users by the end of each Sprint, it ought to be 100% nearly every time."

Stuff always happens.

Sully paused. "See this third Sprint, 'T,' we didn't complete about two-thirds of the work we committed to. The tickets carried over into the next Sprint 'U' where we committed to even more work, including those that carried, and our Predictability Ratio hit 88%!"

"The team really pulled together to make those commitments!" Sully said excitedly, congratulating them.

Continuing, "Look at the next two Sprints where our Predictability Ratio falls to 35%. Why do you suppose that is?"

He paused, and seeing that no one was quick to reply, he said, "To me, it looks like we put a lot of effort into making Sprint 'U' happen and burnt ourselves out. We probably also encountered some big roadblocks in Sprints 'V' and 'W,' too."

He stopped to take a breath.

Jack looked at Sully is disbelief, "You can get all that from this chart?"

Sully replied, "Yes, in combination with the next four reports," *Long pause.*

Sully fessed up, "Plus I cheated a little. I also knew what was happening in each of those Sprints. That helped me fill in a few blanks."

Jack said, "This is priceless!" No one objected.

"That's quite a compliment. I really appreciate it, Jack," Then Sully replied.

"What is 'invaluable' about this report?"

"The Predictability Ratio is based on measurable, historical data. Data we have in Jira about the team's past performance."

"In the past, we've only been able to estimate based on our experience, which is still valuable.

"Unfortunately, opinions are subjective and influenced by individual perceptions, and can be inaccurate due to biases, limited information, misinterpretations, and/or beliefs."

"The Predictability Ratio will be a powerful tool for us in quarterly planning to ensure we commit to the right amount of work," Jack said enthusiastically.

Sully replied, "Yes, and in combination with the Crystal Ball, it will certainly help us plan future quarters."

"We'll still need to rely on our experience to anticipate upside and downside uncertainty, like we do with the Crystal Ball," Jack continued.

"I can also see how it will help guide company strategy," he added.

After identifying the other elements in the chart and fielding a few questions from the team, Sully asked, "Can I move on to the next report?" checking in with his teammates.

"The next report is the Readiness Ratio. While it's primarily geared toward Product Management types, it alerts executives and leaders about possible issues with meeting near-term objectives and provides visibility to those that are involved in early scope discussions. It also provides the team with a quick and easy way to see if we need to perform more or less refinement."

"This report represents the quality of the customer's requirements that are the fuel for our Sprints, and the amount of the work to be done in our backlog. Work that has been defined, understood, and sized by the team, and is *ready* to be worked on."

"It determines if the team has two to three Sprints, or four to six weeks' worth, of work representing customer value in the hopper."

He continued, "The goal is to achieve a balance between too much and too little. The gauge will change color depending on where the metric is."

Aishwarya asked, "What color will it be when we have three Sprints worth of work that is ready?"

"Green is a perfect score. It indicates 100%!"

"What about when it gets low?"

"A lot like your car's gas gauge, when it gets too low it's in the red zone, only in this case this one will not 'squawk' at you when you're about to run out of gas." *Pause.*

Sully checked the faces of his audience. He switched to the team's *live* dashboard to display the team's current Readiness Ratio gauge onto the screen, then continued.

"Unlike our car's gas tank, we can overfill this one. As the needle goes beyond 100%, the gauge turns dark grey."

"Okay, I'll bite," Fin asked, "Why is our current gauge grey?"

"Right now, its grey because we have a lot of old tickets in the backlog that haven't been looked at in more than six months and are probably obsolete."

"Jack is reviewing them and starting the cleanup process. In the interim, I have the task of removing the sizing, or points, from tickets that are older than a year. That will help."

Jack said, "You all can expect to get asked questions about some of the tickets as I review them."

The Readiness Ratio report worked as designed and met its intended purpose.

Now for the remaining three.

Chapter Thirteen

INDICATOR LIGHTS

"**V**isualization gives you answers to questions you didn't know you had."

– Ben Schneiderman

"These next three reports are similar to the indicator lights on your dashboard," Sully was careful not to use the term 'idiot lights' for good reason, "they tell the driver when something is wrong."

"The next two metrics are for Productivity. These are great self–improvement tools for engineering leadership, developers, and process champions, like me. They can be useful to anyone who has an interest in the results of improvements from across the organization at the team level, or in promoting self–managing teamwork."

"They measure how long processes take to complete. The goal is to uncover problems that cause work in progress to slow or stop altogether."

Sully displayed a chart on the screen.

"**The *Cycle Time* report** measures our teams' productivity, or how efficiently we're completing work. Specifically, the average time a ticket takes to complete once it's been started within a two-week iteration."

"It's a common report. It's relatively easy to measure and understand. Wouldn't you agree?" Sully concluded.

He saw several heads nod yes.

Then Elli spoke up, "a couple of the bars are more than ten days, the length of a Sprint. What does that indicate?"

"The tall bars show us that the tickets that were completed in that Sprint took longer than ten days on average. With some investigation, I'd bet many of those carried over from the previous Sprint, and there were probably a couple that took much longer than the two Sprints, skewing the average."

"I think I had one of those tickets," Elli said. She appeared satisfied with the explanation.

Sully stopped to take a swig of water before moving on.

"**Which leads** me to the next productivity metric, ***Work in Progress***, or WIP. The WIP report reveals, in more detail, how long each process historically took to complete between *start* and *finish*."

Sully had learned about WIP from Leland in his Lean Six training.

Sully pulled up a before and current picture of the chart on the screen.

"Here, each process is shown as a line. Peaks indicate something took more time than usual and tell us we ought to investigate the circumstances or root cause to find out if there is an impediment that's slowing us down that we can mitigate or remove altogether."

"Valleys indicate tickets took less time. We want all these lines to be flat and low or trending down."

Sully looked at the faces around the room. Niko was curious.

"We're looking at before and now, correct?" asked Niko. Sully nodded in agreement.

"There's a red line near the top of the *before* graph which looks to have an average of about eight-days. It's missing in the current one. It disappeared," Niko attempted cleverly.

"I was hoping someone would ask about that," Sully had put the bait on the hook, "That was the Ganesh's Approval step we removed last month that was gating and holding up ticket completion until right before the Sprint closed."

"If there are no more questions," he continued, "In the last few minutes, I'd like to share the final report.

"Defects Reported is a powerful report even though it's straightforward. It's useful for executives, leaders, managers, and self-improving teams. It's a metric that reflects the quality of our development process, *considering* product quality. It tracks the number of defects reported in a time period."

"It's so much more than that, though. This metric effectively closes a loop between all five reports by adding balance and providing feedback to the other four reports.

"This one is the easiest to find where the *balanced* part comes in," Sully paused for a deep breath.

"It will tell us if quality is improving or degrading based on improvements being made elsewhere in the process."

"Who can tell us an example that should help improve quality?" he paused.

Aishwarya said, "Shift-left testing."

"Test Driven Development," George added.

Niko chimed in with," AI tools to improve code!"

"Better user stories," said Jack.

"Exactly," Sully inquired again, "How about something that could cause defects to increase?"

"I hate when this happens," Aishwarya had a look of embarrassment, "When we miss something critical in a test case or with automated testing."

"Yup, what if we stuffed our Sprints with tickets we didn't understand and had dependencies that were not identified?" Sully challenged.

Elli replied, "I'd expect we'd be spinning our wheels, constantly switching from one task to another and would forget or miss something that could cause a defect."

"Point is, are the defects reported trending down or up, if so, why? Is there something that's not working or are we missing automated tests for a component?" Sully asked rhetorically.

"Or are we trying to move too fast and sacrificing quality at the same time? Or vice-versa?" *Pause.*

Sully scratched his forehead, as if he had instantly become Columbo, "Did we make a change or improvement that is causing more defects?"

He paused for questions.

Since there were none, he concluded, "All five of these reports relate to each other. Impediments we discover in Cycle Time and WIP will affect our Predictability Ratio."

"Thank you, I appreciate your time. A lot of thought and effort went into creating these metrics and these reports, and I am confident that over time, we will take full advantage of them. Have a great day!"

Jack said, "Thank you Sully, nice presentation. I guess we'll see how valuable these metrics and reports are moving forward," as he made his way through the conference room door on his way to the next meeting.

Before the next retrospective meeting, Sully noticed something going on toward the end of the Sprint. Many of the tickets were waiting for peer reviews for more than three days, and most of the work moved into validation status in the last few days of the iteration.

Once the current Sprint closed, the Work in Progress report illustrated both these issues.

He brought up the topics in the next retrospective, displaying the WIP graph on the screen.

Peer reviews typically happened after a developer had written code and indicated it was ready to go. The purpose was to have other developers review the original work to provide feedback and recommend any potential improvements to the code before it was finalized.

After everybody gathered in ACL, Sully pulled up the team's dashboard onto the screen, focusing on the Work in Progress report.

Sully pointed to the In Review line on the graph for the previous Sprint.

"I noticed in our last Sprint, the time to get peer reviews done went through the roof as the recent WIP report shows. What happened?"

They tossed around a few ideas, as well as a few excuses as to why, the most common being lack of attention.

"Team sport," Sully reminds them, "What if we had some timing guidelines? Something you all agree to?"

Niko proposed, "What if we review every ticket within twenty-four hours, could we agree to that?"

"Yeah, then again, what if it's complex and a review takes more time than usual?" added Elli.

She reviewed a lot of tickets and did not want to set herself up for failure.

Fin jumped in, "How about forty-eight hours for those, and the developer had better leave a lot of clues documented in the code to make the review easier. They could also give us a heads-up when one of those is coming up."

In the end, the Cloud team decided to set a team agreement to conduct normal reviews within twenty-four hours and high impact reviews within forty-eight hours, and that occasionally, there would be exceptions.

Sully moved on to the validation traffic jam.

"Aishwarya, now that the Sprint is over, how are you doing?"

"I had hardly anything to validate, then all the tickets came into my queue in the last few days of the Sprint!" Aishwarya was clearly upset and frustrated, "It happens all the time."

Sully nods, "Yea, I noticed that, too. We can see it in the WIP report - see how the line for In Test is high, and how it jumped up in the last Sprint?"

The group nodded.

Aishwarya wanted some relief, and could not wait for Sully to address the team, so she jumped in.

"How could we get tickets to come into In Test all during the Sprint, not just the last few days?"

A few ideas were discussed.

"Maybe we could get the easier tickets done early."

"I think that would leave all the heavy lifting for validation until the end."

"The more difficult tickets are also the riskiest of not being completed by the end of the Sprint."

"If there's a pile-up, what if someone who's completed all their tickets for the Sprint jumps in to lend a hand, so long as they aren't validating their own ticket?"

Eventually, the team agreed on a hybrid approach. If someone had a risky, more complex ticket, they would speak up, letting others know so they could get a few of the easy ones done first.

Additionally, they agreed to an 'all hands' approach as they reached the end of a Sprint. It would give support to Aishwarya, and they would finish together, as a team.

"These are two powerful examples of creating flow," Sully pointed out to his teammates.

Sully was keeping tabs on limiting work in progress. Early in his career, Sully investigated what caused defects and how expensive rework was for an organization. He discovered that generally, people were most effective and efficient when they had two tasks or priorities to work on at any given time.

Leland backed this up during his Lean Six studies.

He was looking at the team's Sprint Board one day and noticed that all the developers had three to five tickets in progress at a time, with one exception, Niko.

Sully brought this up to the team, "Let's consider this example: A developer has only one ticket and is waiting for the machine to build code, a time-consuming process sometimes. Not extremely efficient."

The developers nodded like they agreed it was a pain in the rear to have to wait.

"During that down time, what could they do?" Sully let the question hang in the air for several seconds.

"The dev could have worked on a second ticket instead of twiddling their thumbs, waiting for code to build."

"On the other hand, if you have more than two tickets working at the same time, you are spending more time switching between tasks and have to recall where you last were before starting forward again," explained Sully.

"Focusing on only two tickets at a time will help to increase focus and reduce the number of defects. We all know rework is incredibly expensive. Defects cause interruptions in our flow that can be severe, depending upon who finds them and when. They can also be time consuming to fix, depending on the nature of defect itself."

The team took this to heart and adjusted to working on two pieces of work at a time in the next Sprints, getting more completed in the process.

Perhaps this was Niko's secret sauce to being so productive. Or maybe he was really *that* good.

After a month or two, the three improvements worked like a charm, tickets were flowing in a steady stream and were completed before the end of the iteration.

Finally, The Cloud team have established a steady and predictable flow of development work that can be deployed whenever they choose, meeting their customers' needs on time.

Sully reflected on Elli's advice and was glad he was patient and kept pushing forward.

He vowed to continue coaching the team on achieving a highly productive flow.

The Adaptability Scorecard was an invaluable tool that was intended to supplement Kaplan and Norton's Balanced Scorecard.

It was incredible to uncover everyday issues that were almost undiscoverable, such as issues that were blocking the Cloud team from completing their work, visualizing the team's whereabouts regarding customer requirements, team predictability and performance, as well as product quality.

The quick and easy way to understand data visualizations also helped the team stay informed when improvements went well, when they did not, or when they created unintended consequences.

Think of this the next time you get into your car. There are gauges for fuel, vehicle and engine speed, temperature, oil pressure, and a slew of warning lights that show up when something is malfunctioning. For controls, a steering wheel to change direction, a pedal to increase speed, another to slow down or stop, and a shifter to select forward or backward.

Can you imagine operating a vehicle without gauges or controls? Why would you operate a high-performance team any differently?

Sully reflected on how far they had come together and felt a tremendous sense of accomplishment. At least they were on the road to delivering great products for the new initiative!

Is it sustainable? Sully wondered.

Sustaining valuable outcomes was another road the team had not yet travelled on.

Chapter Fourteen

FINAL DESTINATION

"We are not a team because we work together. We are a team because we trust, respect, and care for each other."

–Vala Afshar

Sully's success with the Cloud team earned him respect throughout the group. He was rewarded with more responsibility as a result.

Typical, he thought. It happened subtly over time.

After having been with Dominion for a year, Sully started working with a second Cloud team. Later, a third was added, a mobile app development team.

On top of it, the Program Management team was cut in half, leaving them struggling to carry out all their responsibilities, including the crucial function of quarterly planning, which usually happened at the last minute.

The team finally relinquished that responsibility completely with no clear replacement in sight to take it on.

Sully recognized the need and reluctantly considered adding this vital task to his overflowing plate.

Sully brought the issue up in his next one-on-one meeting with Carlos in 'L&L,' a smaller conference room named after one of the local food trucks. He sat down at the small conference table, and let out a sigh, concerned that he was about to volunteer for such a huge responsibility.

Carlos asked, "What's up?"

"Program got cut. They're saying they can't do PI planning any more. How could I help?"

Carlos hesitated a bit, rubbing his scruffy jaw in thought.

Despite his concerns, Sully stepped up to the plate anyway, saying, "I'd like to take this on, I have a few improvements in mind. I'm just worried about the additional responsibility."

Carlos suggested, "Why don't you give it a try and see how it goes. If it's too much on your plate, we can redistribute some of your responsibilities."

So, he took on facilitating quarterly planning. Everything, including planning, facilitation, and follow-up.

Sully made a point of asking people in the planning sessions to identify risks and dependencies where issues existed across the tech stack and teams, especially those in different parts of Dominion. All told, there were more than 250 developers from across multiple teams, groups, and divisions.

He developed a strategy in his mind's eye, *we need to develop a high level of collaboration between teams, exactly like the Cloud team did.*

The planning group of 250 people spanned teams across groups and divisions.

For the people collectively resolving customer problems by designing and developing solutions, collaborating would be crucial. In addition, Sully saw firsthand how the collaboration between the members of his original Cloud team had already started to take hold with the other teams and groups around them. He felt good about making such a widespread impact.

Six months later, after the major new initiative started, Carlos asked Sully to take on a fourth team who would be developing the app functionality for the motion detection feature. Sully was anxious this was really going to be taking on too much.

He took a pause. Sully was already working with three scrum teams, and had taken on quarterly planning, which in and of itself was almost a full-time job.

At that point, the original Cloud team was chugging along steadily, efficient and effective, practically self-managing.

The next day, he approached Carlos who was sitting in his cube. Carlos removed his reading glasses.

Sully said, "I'm worried about taking on a fourth team in addition to everything else I'm doing. I'm afraid I'll be neglecting my other responsibilities by stretching myself too thin."

"Let's see how it goes." Carlos was developing a catch phrase.

Meanwhile, in whatever spare time Sully had, he managed to implement the Adaptability Scorecard across six development teams in his group.

Fifteen months later, Sully attended another internal meeting in ACL to review the past quarter's results. Steve was back in town. The software engineering managers shared success stories, failures, and lessons learned with each other, Carlos, Steve, and the division's executive leader, Knox. It was a full house.

Like Carlos and Steve, Knox came to Dominion as part of the start-up acquisition. He stood six foot five inches tall, and was stocky and muscular, suggesting he had been a powerlifter at the gym sometime in his past. He wore reading glasses, had close cut hair and typically wore a long-sleeve office casual dress shirt or Polo over denim jeans or khakis.

Knox was also into cars and even had a Rally race car. Sully had a hard time picturing his large frame fitting inside such a small car like a Subaru WRX.

Despite his intimidating appearance, Sully thought Knox was a positive, likeable character. After an impromptu brainstorming session on visualizing the team's cloud expense data, Sully developed a new respect for Knox, who had a lot of experience and was extremely smart, even though he did not flaunt it.

Knox loved the after-quarter reviews because it meant that the shared lessons learned could turn into improvements for the other teams in his group.

This time, the meeting ended early. As the team managers were filing out of ACL, Knox asked Carlos, Steve, and Sully to stick around.

Sully wasn't sure if he was in trouble or getting a promotion.

Knox was curious about what Sully had done with the Cloud team.

"It's been about 15 months, right," Knox indicated, as he engaged Sully, leaning forward in his chair with his forearms on the conference table.

"The Cloud team has been performing steadily at a high level. How did you do that Sully?" Knox inquired.

Sully felt like he was put on the spot, so he inhaled deeply to gather his thoughts.

Carlos and Steve's body language was encouraging.

"Well, when I first started, I built relationships with the team." Sully was stalling while he assembled a mental outline.

"Realizing there were problems, we started working together with the team to resolve them, one at a time, starting with the low-hanging fruit."

"Where'd you start and why?" Knox asked.

"There was a communication problem between the two halves of the team. They worked opposite hours on the clock. They didn't have time to ask questions and bounce ideas off each other during refinement or even contemplate how they could approach solving the customer's problem."

"Tell me more," said Knox.

"On top of that, the people validating work had to wait until well after their work time the next day to find out how to setup a test and do the validation, there were a lot of unidentified dependencies, and even deployment issues."

"Go on."

"Realizing this, we started to address each issue. The first was the requirements process. If the dev's don't know what problem to solve, they can't. It was *the* starting place, because user stories are the fuel for the development car."

He thought Knox would appreciate the reference.

"With the help of Carlos and others, we added a couple of pre-refinement sessions to review the work to be done ahead of the larger team's final review. It helped provide much needed time to anticipate the other dev's questions and have some thoughts about how to approach a solution."

"What did you do about the QA engineer's problem?" Knox displayed interest.

"Aishwarya suggested we add a field to each Jira ticket where the dev could put notes about how to setup for the test and other tips."

"Sounds simple. What were the results?"

"We cut out the wait-time to start a test, and the typical cycle was cut in half."

"That's exciting! What can you tell us about the dependencies problem?"

"The big ones were stopping work in their tracks, often in the middle of the Sprint. We were relying on dev's from other teams to provide something."

"Knowing engineers like to talk to other engineers, I encouraged them to go find out info about the work we needed, and when it would be ready. The developers started collaborating."

"Funny thing is, I believe they started to gain an understanding of how the overall system fits together, including their piece. So, we got 80% better at identifying and mitigating dependencies, I'd say."

"With some admin help, we also updated our tickets to include a prompt that would remind us to discuss dependencies and other risks for each work item during refinement. Like a training tool to help us make it a habit."

Sully sensed Knox was about to ask about deployments and forged ahead.

"For deployments, it was entirely possible to lose a ticket, and the code that was associated with it, because we were using a manual, copy–n–paste process. Also, Dominion's multiple, sometimes lengthy moratoriums didn't help."

Knox looked worried and recognized the risk, "Okay, how did you all fix this problem?"

"I worked with the team and a Jira admin to design a solution in Jira."

"How's it work?"

"Now, when a Sprint closes, the closed tickets stay on a separate Kanban board that the team uses to manage their Prod deployments. Now that they are automated, the team can essentially deploy whenever they want."

"I'd say there was a better than 50-60% improvement to the overall flow of work, and that the team is much happier."

"Wouldn't you agree, Carlos and Steve?" Sully asked, trying to involve them.

They both nodded their heads in agreement.

"Go on," said Steve.

"In each case, I relied on what I had learned and practiced in the past from my Agile, Project Management, and Lean Six Sigma mentors.

It's also important to note that in each case, involving the team and creating visualizations to support each fix will help each improvement stick. So far, the team has been making smaller continuous improvements to each fix, bringing up issues or suggestions in our retrospectives."

"Great! What can you tell me about the Rally Cry?" Knox had heard his managers raving about it.

"When the new strategy was introduced by Product Management, the team size changed dramatically, and the communication issues we had went away, which was good. The team still worked continuously on the improvements that we had put into place, and we now had more opportunity to consider the work ahead of time."

"What happened next?" inquired Knox.

"As you know, we aligned each team's goals to the new strategy, organizing them around a Rally Cry each team developed for themselves."

"I'd learned about it from a leadership novel years ago, and it has been an incredible way to create alignment between strategy and goals quickly."

"And what were the results, in your opinion?"

"The Cloud team was hit with a 'perfect storm.' New initiative, and an org change that split their team in half and laid off two of their friends. It's enough to put any team into a major skid and go off the track."

"There is no hard data to point to. I believe the Rally Cry helped them focus on the work, and they evolved quickly into a high-performing team again!"

"I agree wholeheartedly!" said Carlos.

"Unfortunately, there was still something keeping work from flowing from the backlog to production, similar to a clogged fuel filter in a car. The engine still runs, only not at its peak performance," Sully was hoping one of them would ask about his Adaptability Scorecard.

"Tell us more about the charts in the deck," Steve chimed in eagerly.

"We needed a way to visualize all the data we're capturing in Jira, to drive improvement. Making a small set of good metrics visible are key tenets of Agile and Lean."

He looked directly at Knox, "Can you picture driving your race car if it didn't have a few gauges to tell you about the car's health?"

"Obviously, no," replied Knox.

He felt a little like Sully was calling him out.

"After extensive research, I defined five metrics. The first was a chart that could help us develop Predictability. Then a gauge to help us keep an eye on the health of requirements, the Readiness Ratio. Two more to expose non-apparent issues to improve Productivity, and the last to track Defect reporting rates to keep everything in check. The objective of the Adaptability Scorecard system is to help the team achieve a sustainable flow of value to its customers."

"The deck only contained one of the charts, where are the others?" Steve looked curious.

"The Predictability Ratio/Activity report was shown in the presentation. I bet you noticed that the Cloud team's metric was the highest and flat."

"I did. In fact, they look super steady, and they are maintaining a solid pace. The other teams were improving, and only one team was still experiencing ups and downs," Steve said leaning back in his chair.

"One of the last to get the set of reports was the motion app team, and I'm working with their manager to improve the way the people on the team work some of their processes," explained Sully.

Steve wanted to know more about the Cloud team's performance.

"I noticed the Cloud team has been performing at that steady pace for several quarters now."

Sully replied, "We've been working together the longest, and they were the first to get the reports."

"And, thanks to Steve's capacity planner, we effectively paired velocity with capacity," Sully said, looking at them.

"It's a spreadsheet Sully and I put together," Steve added, then continued.

"The Crystal Ball has improved Sprint planning and predictability tremendously. We now add the right amount of work to make our Sprint goal and stretch a little, without overloading the developers for each Sprint."

Sully chimed in, "The work in Sprints is well known, thanks to the improvements we'd made to the requirements process. Quarterly planning is a little different because there is more uncertainty. The Crystal Ball helps reduce that and supports our estimations."

"The two metrics for Productivity measure the time it takes for processes to complete. Particularly, the WIP report was instrumental in helping us discover delays in the peer review and validation processes."

"What was the solution for those?" Carlos asked, leaning forward, already knowing the answer Sully would deliver.

"Once we knew the issues, the team problem-solved and determined two new team agreements. One for a 24 to 48 hours for a peer review turnaround, and another to swarm on validations if a pile developed."

"Now, the team has a sustainable, steady flow."

"Nice. How did the Cloud team achieve the overall pace?" asked Knox.

"It took time and patience. If the other improvements hadn't been made, it wouldn't have been possible for the team to perform at this level."

"The Readiness Ratio is another key report. It really helped us maintain the right amount of work to be done, fully refined and ready to go in the product backlog."

"In fact, the Cloud team has consistently maintained that metric at 100%, near perfect over the Sprints in the past five quarters." *Long pause.*

Sully reflected for a moment; *The Cloud team has come a long way on their journey since I joined them three years ago.*

Now, they were significantly better at preparing for each Sprint.

They attacked problems together.

They used the metrics to make data-informed decisions for improvements in their retrospectives.

And team morale was at an all-time high.

Sully was ready to conclude, "The five engineers on the Cloud team are now completing 30% more work than the original team of 15. Occasionally it's as high as 50%!"

Steve could not contain himself, "That's incredible Sully!"

They rapidly approached the end of the official meeting time.

"When will my teams get these reports?" Steve had an urgency in his voice.

"I've started to implement them for your teams this week, and plan to coach your Scrum Master on how to work with the team and use them. It may take some time, so patience is appreciated."

Knox wanted more, "Where can I look at the other reports for each team?"

"I'll send all of you the links to each team's dashboard later today." Additionally, I'm working on reports for you that roll up the individual team's metrics into a single group composite."

As they were getting up from their seats in the conference room, Steve said, "Let me know how I can help."

"Good stuff, Sully," chimed Carlos.

Knox said, "Nice work, Sully. The Predictability chart is absolute gold, especially with the four other reports. If I can do anything for you, reach out. I'm eager to see what you come up with for the Cloud cost visuals, too.

Later that afternoon, Carlos and Steve cornered Knox and grabbed the L&L conference room, standing around the four-person table like an upside-down three-legged stool.

Carlos said, "Steve and I have been talking about the job Sully has been doing for us."

"His results with the Cloud team are phenomenal, and he's taken on a lot more responsibility, gracefully working with four teams and facilitating quarterly planning from A to Z."

"We think Dominion ought to promote him., and if we can find the budget, get him a team he could lead to replicate the results across more teams."

Knox spoke up, "I've been thinking the same thing this afternoon."

"Also, with the cost savings that come out of teams being more effective and efficient, the budget shouldn't really be an issue," Steve added.

Knox concluded, "Alright, sounds like we are in agreement. Why don't you both come up with a plan in the next week and let me know what it'll take."

Well, Sully did not know if that last part really happened or not. His amazing success in freeing Dominion's teams to become 30% more productive and consistently over 80% predictable would sure be worthy of it.

As Sully walked back to his desk after the meeting with Knox, he couldn't help but reflect on the winding path that had brought him here. Twenty years of lessons, starting in his father's driveway in Medford where he first learned that fixing things meant understanding systems, not just symptoms. His dad had taught him to listen to an engine, to feel where it struggled, to trace problems back to their source. Those early lessons in mechanical diagnostics had evolved into something far more complex—diagnosing and fixing human systems.

Every mentor along the way had added another tool to his kit. His Agile coaches had shown him how to make work visible and iterative. His Project Management mentors had taught him to see the big picture while managing the details. His Lean Six Sigma training had given him the discipline to measure, analyze, and improve. Scott had demonstrated the power of asking the right questions instead of providing all the answers. Each lesson had been a component, waiting to be assembled into something greater.

What he'd accomplished with the Cloud team—transforming fifteen struggling engineers into five high-performers who delivered 30% more value—wasn't magic. It was the culmination of two decades of learning applied with patience and precision. He'd taken a team drowning in miscommunication, missed dependencies, and manual processes, and systematically rebuilt them into a predictable, productive, self-improving unit. The Adaptability Scorecard, the Rally Cry, the collaborative culture – they were all manifestations of lessons learned and refined over years.

Looking ahead, Sully felt a familiar excitement. The same feeling he'd had as a young mechanic when he'd finally diagnosed a particularly stubborn problem. But now, instead of one engine to fix, he had the opportunity to transform entire organizations. The success with the Cloud team wasn't an ending—it was proof that the methodology worked, a blueprint he could carry forward. Whatever came next, whether promotion or simply more teams to guide, Sully knew he had built something repeatable, something that could scale. The Process Mechanic had found his rhythm, and he was just getting started.

Afterword

"It's not the strongest or the most intelligent who will survive, but those who can best manage change."

– Charles Darwin

Wow, what a ride! Sully went on to deploy the Adaptability Scorecard for a total of six teams in the division and create a set of reports for group executives that rolled up the data from multiple teams.

Executives and leaders, you want to see your strategies come to life. There's a lot riding on them. You need product development teams that are *predictable* and can deliver brilliant products and features in a timely manner. You have hired a highly intelligent workforce. Maybe it is time to unleash their power.

Agile, Change, and Project Managers, you want to serve your teams so they can deliver those products in an efficient and effective way, so they contribute to the company coffers.

Developers, you want to solve customer problems by designing and creating solutions that delight your customers. You want to ply your craft without process impeding progress.

The Process Mechanic, *Adaptability Scorecard*™ reports companion is a primer for you and your teams.

Use the right tool for the right job at the right time. To solve any organizational issue, first, you must understand your context, culture, and the situation you find yourself in.

Are your teams unpredictable? Are they able to adapt to the rapidly changing marketplace?

Your relationships matter. Your people will assist you in improving the situation and circumstances you find yourself in. If you haven't already, start by fostering extraordinary relationships and trust. To do this, include the people on your teams in problem solving, follow through on what you say you will do, and run experiments with them to discover the best solutions for your customers and the people in your organization.

Communicate effectively with those you work with. The best thing you can do is tell a person they are important to you. Give them your time and attention. Listen actively, hearing with attention and understanding. Put down your device, get away from the monitor, and avoid thinking of your next question or a snappy comeback. Building relationships by communicating and listening effectively builds trust.

Ask someone who is smarter and more experienced to help identify what is standing in the way.

Collaborate with your people; they are the closest to the problems in your process and already have devised potential solutions. Seek their expertise. Engaging the people with boots on the ground creates ownership. They will own the solution and improve it continuously so that it endures. Why not tap into their insights?

Start the conversation by being curious and asking great questions, such as, "Based on your perspective, how could we solve this?" or better yet, "How did someone else fix this?" "Why does this process exist?" "How can we make the solution better?" "Tell me more." If there are differing subjective opinions, "Could we run an experiment?"

By understanding process problems, including why and what was done in the past to fix them, you can move forward and choose the best process or tool to improve and try it out! Aim to provide some guardrails. In other words, avoid processes that are too restrictive with a lot of unnecessary overhead. Free your developers to do what they love to do every day!

At the beginning, the team in our story was unpredictable. You watched them overcome several obstacles, one at a time, to develop flow and predictability.

Among the obstacles described, requirements is the most important. Without great requirements coming from customers and users, it will be difficult for development organizations to create solutions for problems they cannot understand. They will miss the mark almost 100% of the time. 'Almost' is equivalent to getting lucky. Like playing the lottery. Who wants to risk that?

If you as a Scrum Master or Project Manager think 'Product Management' is not my area or job, think again. Get familiar with it. Your Product Managers and/or Product Owners need to be your closest friends. If they are not, make them so.

Planning improves dramatically by pairing historical velocity with capacity, leading to predictability. It aligns commitments with capacity at all levels of the organization. Stakeholders gain visibility into achievable goals. Teams adapt to sprint variations without risking outcomes, enabling them to deliver predictably in dynamic conditions.

There is little doubt that the Adaptability Scorecard is a powerful tool. It uses available data to help people make important decisions and solve problems in your context. The reports visualize the data in a simple, yet easy to understand way. They help to monitor the system as improvements are made. This in turn enables teams to become self-improving and systems to effectively support execution of leadership's strategies.

In the story, team size and location both affect communication and collaboration greatly. Find out more in the companion.

In the end, the team achieves a very predictable flow of customer value.

Want to know which metrics in the book drove real team consistent Predictability of 80% with a third of the developers?

Discover more about the reports from our story in the reports companion.

We will illustrate how the five reports of the Adaptability Scorecard are an invaluable addition to Kaplan and Norton's Balanced Scorecard. The two work together and interconnect to create a 'balance' that drives customer and employee satisfaction. They also stimulate improvements that add to top-line revenue and reduce cost to increase a company's bottom-line.

The companion looks at the nuts and bolts of the Adaptability Scorecard. We'll cover the Predictability Ratio, The Readiness Ratio, Cycle Time, Work in Progress, and Defects Reported reports in more depth, why each is important, and how to interpret each one.

The Process Mechanic, *Adaptability Scorecard* reports companion is a primer for you and your teams. If you haven't read it already, get your copy and read it today!

Beyond the Adaptability Scorecard, I question why self-organizing teams are not more prevalent. Perhaps that is a story for another day.

Acknowledgements

I appreciate you, Kathy Lansford. Your energy and advice are invaluable. You tirelessly corrected my grammar, use of the written word, and sloppy punctuation with a smile in your heart and on your face. If you wanted a second career, this could be it.

Sean Van Tyne, my favorite CX/UX expert. Dude, you are such a nut for Scorecards! Your excitement became my inspiration! Sean is the nonfiction author of *The Customer Experience Revolution* and *Easy to Use 2.0*.

Will Simpson for coaching me on 'how-to' publish and market an Indie book, giving so selflessly what you had learned to help me get started, and avoid the 'experience' of learning the hard way. Will is the fiction author of *You've Got to Lose to Win."*

Special mention to those who freely gave of their time, advice, and critical feedback in the final hours; Steve Harper, Scott Killen, William Baxter, Steve Burke, and La'Quyet Brooks.

The people at eazyBI who tirelessly answered my seemingly endless string of questions while developing the custom reports.

The incredible people I had the privilege of working with over the previous 25 years: the executives, managers, and engineers. You are all inspired leaders. I thoroughly enjoyed working with each of you. Together, with your support and leadership, we accomplished some extraordinary things.

Finally, this book and this story are dedicated to the professional engineers I worked with throughout my past, whose managers told them exactly what to do, by when, and how. Beaten down by the system, I would see them hunkered down in their cubicles, hoping they would not be out looking for another job after the next quarter's layoff. My heart goes out to you. You are brilliant, do not stop believing in your talent and ability to solve problems! It is there, even if it is lurking in the background.

About the author

The Process Mechanic™ - *A Self-Improving Team Story* was inspired by real experience and events working alongside technical product developers building solutions for real customers. Indeed, this team achieved unencumbered flow and became *predictable* and *self-improving.*

Robert Woodcock has a lifetime of experience working with development teams building technical products. Together, they have increased product revenue by over six times in less than two years, reduced bottom line costs by over $15.7 million, and increased team productivity by over 30% with a third of the developers.

Robert's journey began after attending college, where he realized years later, he was good, no incredible, at turning ordinary teams into extraordinary ones by involving and inspiring people to create improvements that endure. His first team increased year over year revenue by 1.7 times in only six months!

Driven by the desire to create environments that engineers want to come to every day, today he guides the way small and medium businesses operate to get more out of their product development engine and is a part-time author.

"No one can whistle a symphony. It takes a whole orchestra to play it." – Halford E.

Learn more about Robert Woodcock and The Process Mechanic™ at theprocessmechanic.com